Winds of Fury,
CIRCLES OF GRACE

Winds of Fury,
CIRCLES OF GRACE
Life After the Palm Sunday Tornadoes

DALE CLEM

Abingdon Press
Nashville

WINDS OF FURY, CIRCLES OF GRACE

Copyright © 1997 by Abingdon Press

All rights reserved.

This book is printed on recycled, acid-free, elemental-chlorine-free paper.

Cataloging-in-Publication data has been applied for.
ISBN: 0-687-01795-5

Scripture quotations, unless otherwise noted, are from the New Revised Standard Version Bible, copyright © 1989, by the Division of Christian Education of the National Council of the Churches of Christ in America. Used by permission.

Scripture quotations noted NKJV are from The New King James Version. Copyright © 1979, 1980, 1982, Thomas Nelson Inc., Publishers.

Quotations noted NIV are taken from the *Holy Bible: New International Version.* Copyright © 1973, 1978, 1984 by the International Bible Society. Used by permission of Zondervan Bible Publishers.

"With Kit, Age 7, at the Beach" (p. 106) is from *Stories That Could Be True,* copyright © 1978 William Stafford. Used by permission of the estate of William Stafford.

Excerpt from "Losers" (p. 190) in *Smoke and Steel* by Carl Sandburg, is copyright 1920 by Harcourt Brace & Company and renewed 1948 by Carl Sandburg, reprinted by permission of Harcourt Brace & Company.

interior book design by J. S. Laughbaum

97 98 99 00 01 02 03 04 05 06—10 9 8 7 6 5 4 3 2 1

MANUFACTURED IN THE UNITED STATES OF AMERICA

In memory of my beloved daughter

Hannah Kathryn Clem
July 21, 1989–March 27, 1994

and the nineteen others who died
at the Goshen United Methodist Church

Earl Abbott
Jonathan Abbott
Freddie Bass
Ethelene Blair
David Kuykendall
Michael Mode
Cathy Mode
Zachary Mode
Diane Molock
Ruth Peek
Cicero Peek
George Scroggin
Kirk Scroggin
Eric Thacker
Derek Watson
Kay Watson
Jessica Watson
Marcus "Buddy" Woods
Amy Woods

CONTENTS

FOREWORD

REYNOLDS PRICE

When Dale Clem came to my office at Duke University two years ago, he was not entirely a stranger to me. Though he and his wife had been graduate students at Duke a few years earlier, we'd never previously met (Divinity Schools and their neighboring English Departments are not always in steady communication). But I—like a great many Americans—had learned of Clem's, his family's, and his community's tragic loss in a spring tornado that struck an Alabama church in 1994. I knew that Clem and his minister wife, Kelly Clem, had lost the elder of their two young daughters in the lethal storm; and while I've never had children of my own, I've often felt genuine wonder at the strength of those parents who can literally survive the death of a loved child.

So I was ready to hear Dale's story—the events of one catastrophic weekend and his subsequent hunt for sufficient navigational skills to continue his course through an active life. As he narrated his memories to me, over a number of meetings, I began to sense that he did not yet possess a completed story to tell me or the world. He was still in the eye of his agony. And when he introduced me to Kelly a few weeks later, I felt the same two things about her—she clearly possessed extraordinary self-mastery at the same time as she retained, honestly within her mind, a daunting incompleteness. As Dale insists, so rightly in this book, he and Kelly were far past the inevitable but infantile question *Why? Why me? Why now?* But they had not yet hauled themselves out of the final deep trenches of their scalding encounter with the greatest of mysteries—unearned suffering, the apparent punishment of the unquestionably guiltless.

It would insult their patent honesty to say that this book proves that Dale and Kelly Clem have now cobbled together a finished tale to tell us. The tale of any one of our lives ends only at the moment of death. Indeed, many of us hope that it continues beyond earthly sight and hearing. But what runs so arrestingly through this written account of Dale Clem's pain and slowly advancing recovery is the core wisdom and strength with which he affirms that the main hope of continuance in the face of ultimate pain and loss is the courage to confront the immensity of loss and grief.

In a passage that should strike us all powerfully, Clem says, "For me, healing has come as I lean toward the pain. The hole which causes so much pain is also the source of healing and wholeness. . . . I get in trouble when I pretend it isn't there." In the face of such strength, it seems very likely that the remainder of Clem's life will complicate and enrich the line of the story he finally tells. Meanwhile, the reader can hope that he and Kelly and their second daughter, Sarah, continue their course together and that their present findings in the abyss of death and silence only continue to grow and deepen in the direction so apparent here. Any hardened battlefield hero could learn volumes from them.

PREFACE

Any sorrow can be borne if a story can be told about it.

—Isak Dinesen

On Palm Sunday of 1994, a tornado killed Hannah, my lively, energetic little girl. When I look back, I realize how truly blessed Kelly, Sarah, and I have been with the love and care so many people have shared with us. Many people have stood around us absorbing our pain. What a rare gift it has been to have friends and strangers who have shared our lives and mysteriously absorbed our pain. This book is the result of the pain within me, which was screaming to come out. It was through writing that I was able to work out my grief and reach a greater understanding of faith and suffering.

After the tragedy, I began to read the scores of books about grief and tragedy. Although the stories told of deep pain, I regretted that they didn't express how bad I really felt. I had hoped to take up the pen and express that pain, but that was not possible. If I were able to express that kind of pain, only the grieving would believe it, and the rest would think it insane. Although it angered me when friends told me the pain would go away over time and that "the clock is ticking," I can testify that the disabling pain has indeed subsided into a distant, nightmarish memory, leaving me with a deep, tender wound that I expect to carry always.

This story is also about a God who sustains us. For those experiencing grief, I hope this book can be hopeful and healing. You are not alone. For those who have cared or still do care for the grieving, I hope this book will give you some clues to what the grieving person experiences but can't often express.

Throughout telling the story, I have interspersed some reflections on what I have learned, which I think will give the reader a break from the intensity of the story. The healing insights helped me through the grief journey. As I retell the story, sometimes my writing is very emotive and choppy. I chose not to change that style, for it authentically portrays the pain of those first days and months. As I reflect upon the events, a year later, my writing style is more relaxed, and yet I hope it has its own challenging intensity.

Memories, theology, and certainly this project all have limits. We live in a world where there are always exceptions to the rules. We think we have something figured out, and then we realize that our reasoning isn't always true, or that our minds make incorrect assumptions. I have written this story mainly from my memory, and through rereading newspaper accounts and TV news stories. People in the Goshen United Methodist Church have been gracious to share with me their remembrances, as well as their friendship. I am grateful for all those who have shared and wept with me in holy times of remembering.

I want to thank anyone who heard about the tragedy and was moved to pray, write, send gifts, or call. We always felt love from you and this gave us strength to go on. For your thoughts we are truly thankful.

This book would never have been written without the encouragement given to me by our district superintendent, Herb Williamson, and Bishop Robert Fannin. The Wesley Foundation Board and the students at Jacksonville State University were gracious to let me pursue this dream. Ed Dixon, the Ministerial Educational Leave Society, and the many words of encouragement from friends gave me the courage and opportunity to actually write. But it was my wife Kelly who said, "Dale, stop talking about it and just do it." That finally convinced me to take the time off and begin to write. Our United Methodist Committee on Relief (UMCOR) was helpful to us throughout the tragedy and is responsible for helping us heal in many ways. I am indebted to Steve Long of Duke University's Divinity School for allowing me to be a Duke fellow during February 1995 and 1996. It was at Duke that Reynolds Price was gracious to read what I had written and encourage me to start over, admonishing me, "Just tell the story and stop preaching." I fear I didn't take his advice completely, but I tried. I am honored that he agreed to write the foreword. Fred and Kristin Herzog have been dear friends for years, and were exceptionally kind and encouraging. Fred offered to give me his "professional" opinion. He died before I could take him up on his offer. This work is weaker for lack of the advice his sharp mind could have provided. In May of 1995, I spoke at a reunion of the Academy for Spiritual Formation sponsored by the Upper Room. Some of this material was sharpened by the feedback I received from that experience. I also appreciate Tom and Ann Marie Langford, and Greg Jones for reading the entire manuscript and offering suggestions.

This work would not have been completed without the encouragement and skills of a wonderful proofreader, Opal Lovett. My wife Kelly's deep commitment to this project was a great gift. She and my daughter Sarah made many sacrifices so that I could escape to write. Kelly's strength and wisdom constantly amaze and inspire me to be a better person. Kelly and Sarah's love and patience give me hope for my future and for future generations. This hope and love was embodied in the birth of Laurel Hope Clem in August of 1996. I remain in awe when I see the mysterious life-force God has put into all creation to start over and re-create.

The Ever Widening Circle of Grace

At the one-year anniversary of the tornado, I come to the beach at Gulf Shores to reflect upon what I have learned from this past year. I throw a shell into the water and watch the circles expand. The shell sinks to the sandy bottom, but the ripples from the splash continue outward. I hope that Kelly and I will have the emotional health and support to expand the circles of our experience and life. The alternative would be that the action in the water would become a sinkhole that would suck us into despair, robbing us of all hope and faith. The outward movement toward others and God keeps us balanced.

More than a dozen reporters have asked Kelly and me in the past few weeks what we have learned from this past year. In some ways, they have been guides, forcing us to stop and reflect on our feelings and thoughts.

I walk along the beach, hoping to draw some strength and insight from the sea. As I close my eyes, the sound of the powerful waves is overwhelming.

What have I learned this year? The obvious answers crash down like the noisy waves some forty feet away. I know the deep pain of loss, and have experienced the shock that carried us on. I learned how impatient I was without ordinary conveniences of modern life such as silverware and a microwave. I learned that the red wheelbarrow of faith held me steady, along with God's grace and God's people.

I close my eyes and remember the young reporter just out of college sitting on our living room sofa. She tilted her head to the left and asked with a cheery voice, "So, what's this year been like for you?" The question shot a pain in my stomach. The tone of her voice was the same one might use when asking a child if she enjoyed going to Disney World. A child might say "yes" but only because she feels the adult demands an answer. It is hard to be objective when you are still living in the process. And like the child who feels the demand to answer the question, I responded, "A lot!" I wanted to reply, "Even if I could express this past year in words, I don't think you could understand." I chose not to be obnoxious. I told her about the importance of intentionally loving and having fun with those you love. I told her how we appreciated the tremendous amount of support we had received. She was the fourth reporter to ask a similar question that day. As I listen to the ocean, I think about how I answered the question.

I sit down in the sand about six feet from where the waves create fleeting wet semicircles. In the half light, the wave-prints look like sheets of reflective glass on the sand. I close my eyes again and listen to the surf. The waves crashing far from my bare feet are the loudest. These sounds are distant and comforting. I can breathe deeply and allow the rhythm to rock my inner and outer self.

Nearer to me are softer splashes as the shallow water glides toward me, then recedes. These sounds frighten me, and I open my eyes. From past experience, I know that trusting the surf can become a wet experience. I close my eyes again and again, trying to trust that the gentle waves will not reach me. These softer and more subtle sounds bring shells and other gifts to the shore.

My answers to the reporters were honest, but they didn't address the many questions that remain. The answers were like the loud waves crashing forty feet away, completing the question, "What have I really learned this year?" It is hard to trust the significance of little insights that come to mind.

It is difficult to answer. Dare I admit that I don't have it all figured out? If I say with confidence that I learned this or that, will I create a facade that we are now in control and have it all together? I remember the starched collars and suits that the bishop and district superintendent wore the day after the tornado and how out of place they looked in contrast to the devastation all around us. Even by giving *any* answer to *any* question, or by writing, am I attempting to control my circumstances or to avoid the reality that I am living in the face of uncertainties—in the midst of paradox? Do I simply attempt to play the role of a brave soldier who coldly and rationally speaks of the dead and tries to put the battle behind him to return to the front line? I wonder if my motive to tell the story is feeding my ego. Or is telling the story part of the way I have chosen to deal with the pain and work on healing? I wonder if by attempting to bring closure to the year I am trying to cut it off so that I can get on with the future and put the past behind me. I decide that perhaps it is all of the above. Dare I take the risk?

I fear that by saying that I have learned from living through this tragedy I could be reducing it to something that "makes sense" and is explainable. This cause-and-effect way of looking at the world oversimplifies the contradictions inherent in the world and in ourselves. Yet in that tension lie many of life's truths, which we use to make meaning for our lives.

Any experience, especially one that takes us to the depths, is simply too big for words. Words lessen the experience. Why must we try to explain mystery? Many people have told me that the tornado hit the church and killed Hannah because it gave Kelly and me an opportunity to witness to our faith. I can't accept this; I simply try to live in the mystery. It is tempting to try to explain away the mysteries of life.

In the face of disaster and death, silence may be the only appropriate response. Even telling the stories, much less reflecting on them, somehow takes away their mystery. I do not want to diminish the absurdity of the tragedy, but we have moved on. One year later we are in a different place.

The act of writing about suffering does not imply that suffering needs to be meaningful. I appreciate the response the

Jewish leader gave when asked if there was any meaning in the Holocaust: "I hope not." Writing has helped me remember and reflect upon my experience. I don't think it makes the suffering meaningful—but simply more real. If by sharing my experience another is helped to express his or her feelings, then the writing is healing—and perhaps a meaningful experience for him or her. It could also soften the heart toward compassion. I find the stories of people who have suffered particularly inspiring, for I hope I can respond with humor and dignity the way others have. But suffering itself is not meaningful.

I write the following pages with the hope that I will continue to grow and live outward into the ever widening circles of God's grace. I throw a shell in the surf. Circular ripples expand wider and wider, like each of us in God's wider mystery.

The Call

"There's been a call. Pull over and park." I was driving a vanload of students to a picnic, and our host, Phil, motioned for me to join him in his van. I was confused, but climbed into the passenger seat in his van. "There's been a tornado," he said. "It hit your wife's church. There are some injuries and some deaths. Kelly is in the hospital, the girls are okay; you need to call home." I looked around; the weather was fine in Lawton, Oklahoma. Then it hit me that we were a long way from Piedmont, Alabama.

I leaned forward, trying to figure out if the sounds I was hearing were the words my mind was slowly beginning to comprehend. They couldn't be. "What?" I asked.

Phil slowly repeated the message. "We've had a call. A tornado hit your wife's church. There are injuries and deaths. You need to call this number." He looked at a piece of paper, "A Mr. Christian called."

He handed me the number, and I tried to call it using his cellular phone. "You've got to push 'send,' " he told me.

"When?" I asked him. "When did a tornado hit?"

He said, "I guess it was during worship today."

The phone was busy. I tried the number to my house, but no one answered. I tried calling our neighbor's number, but it was busy.

He said, "Let's just sit here a minute, and you can try again." We couldn't drive, because the cellular phones wouldn't work in some areas of the park. I felt a gnawing ache in my stomach as the news started sinking in.

Phil's secretary had gone into the office and heard a message on the answering machine. I knew it was a miracle that anyone checked that machine before that evening, when we had planned to return.

I tried several more times and finally got through. Mr. Christian's voice was shaky and emotional. "Kelly is going to be okay. She is at the hospital. Sarah is fine."

"How about Hannah?" I asked.

He paused for what seemed like an infinite second or two and said, "I don't know about Hannah, but Sarah is here playing."

As if to be sure I was hearing what I thought I was hearing, I repeated his words back to him. I asked, "What happened? Who died?"

He slowly and emotionally said something like, "I don't know Dale, everything is just crazy. There are trees and houses all down, and lots of people are hurt. We just don't know much yet. It's a mess."

I could tell by the tone of his voice that he was really shaken up about it. I naively asked if I needed to come home, and he said, "Yes."

The connection was fuzzy, and as I searched to push the "end" button I wondered why I was hanging up so quickly. Finally, I had reached a source of information, and I had hung up.

I did not fully comprehend the reality of the tragedy that had just struck our church and family. My question, "Do I need to come home?" was that part of myself that kept saying, "It can't be that bad, and if it is, I'm not sure I want to face it." I wondered, "If they can't find Hannah, where is she?" Surely they would not have left her; I'm sure someone has her and they are taking care of her. A thousand questions raced through my mind.

It was here that a sacred space was created in my heart. I closed my eyes and imagined picking Hannah up over my head and twirling her around. She smiled and squealed with

joy and we hugged. In the months and years since the tragedy, I have often closed my eyes and found myself in that
sacred space uniting a father and his firstborn daughter.

The students gathered around me, and I told them that a
tornado had hit the church, that Kelly and Sarah were injured
but okay, but they didn't know about Hannah. The students
let out a collective moan. I could see the terror in their eyes.
The depth of the students' response grazed a place of previously untouchable pain in my inner being, but I could not
give in to my feelings. Not yet, at least. I went with Phil, the
campus minister, to a private place to learn more details and
make arrangements to leave.

The students I had taken on this spring break service-
learning trip called off the picnic and headed back to the
Wesley Foundation, a United Methodist campus ministry at
Cameron University in Lawton, Oklahoma. Phil did not
drive slowly on our trip back. I buckled up and kept calling
every phone number I could recall. The answering machine
at the Wesley Foundation at Jacksonville State University,
where I was the director and campus minister, picked up. I
heard my secretary's voice, "Dale has been notified in Oklahoma, and Kelly and the girls are okay." What was my
secretary doing coming into work on a Sunday? I was confused, but thought, "Something big must be going on."

My mind and my heart were engaged in a struggle I could
barely contain within myself. My mind kept playing over the
answering machine message, "Kelly and the girls are okay."
My heart was resonating with the fear sparked when Mr.
Christian told me that they didn't know about Hannah. My
heart responded, "She's the strongest four-year-old I know.
My child is invincible." Yet the gnawing, sick feeling continued churning in my stomach.

I called my sister in Huntsville and talked to my nephew
who said that his mom and stepfather had already left to find
Kelly. He said he did not know about Hannah or Sarah, and
the Red Cross said everyone in the church was accounted for

but me. He said that people were calling his house wanting to know more.

As we walked into the Wesley office in Lawton, we learned that the secretary had found Kelly. I called the number and explained to the nurse who I was. I remember that she was very calm and spoke with level-headed compassion. I waited a long time before Kelly answered. As I waited, Kelly was seated on a stretcher in the emergency room, taking deep breaths as she mustered the courage to tell me the dreaded truth. "What do you know?" she asked.

"A tornado hit the church; you and Sarah are okay, but I don't know about Hannah." As I finished, I took a deep breath and realized that tears were running down my cheeks. I feared the worst.

She said in a straight voice, "Hannah is dead."

I will never forget what Kelly said next. "I'm so sorry to tell you over the phone."

"What happened?" I asked. Kelly continued with a touch of panic in her voice, "She was just crushed by heavy blocks and concrete beams. I tried to get her out, but the beams were too heavy. Dale, I tried so hard to move those beams, but they were just too heavy. When we finally dug her out, I patted her and told her I was there and it would be okay. They took her away. She didn't look bad, Dale. I don't think she suffered."

I told her I was sorry that she had to go through such a thing. I was trying to imagine her helpless feeling of not being able to move big concrete blocks and beams off of Hannah. I asked, "Who else died?"

"Oh, you don't want to know. It is really bad. Please come home."

I asked if anyone was with her, and she said that minister friends were taking good care of her. I told her my flight plans, and she assured me that she or someone would meet me. She told me to gather my friends around me to care for me. We both said, "I love you" and hung up.

I went into Phil's private office, where my world stopped.
I broke down and cried.

I imagine myself hanging,
dangling from a rope
spinning around out of control.
I see a blowtorch above me burning the fibers of the rope.
Will all the fibers of my life be charred by the flame?
Will the burning sever my life rope?
Grief descended upon me like a cloak of numbness. Later I would
think of this protective blanket of numbness as a wonderful grace.
It becomes a passageway to the retreat into a hidden room deep
within us. Calling it simply "shock" seems to rob it of its significance. It may be natural to be in shock after a death, but it is not
every day we find ourselves there. While in this room, we hear
talking, but the sounds are muffled and distant. Is there cotton in
my ears? Grief makes you feel as though you are a thousand miles
from the person trying to speak to you. When the person hugs you,
your arms feel like those of an unresponsive, limp rag doll. A good
friend or family member seems like a stranger. But the biggest
stranger is the one who bears your name. For death robs us of our
identity, so that we become strangers even to ourselves.
Back in Piedmont, upon entering the house I notice a brown
hanging plant by the window. I walk over to it. Brown, dead, it's
gone. When did it die? I wonder. How could I not have noticed?
Was it a slow or quick death? I had meant to water it. Perhaps it
was the chill through the window? It's funny how things die before
we notice. I am always surprised when parts of myself have died.
It is as though I wake up and realize that I've changed. I'm not as
I was last year, last month. Often someone else has to notice first.
"You aren't laughing anymore. Don't you remember how you used
to laugh and smile?"
"Oh," I reply, "I hadn't noticed . . . Yes, I remember."

"You don't laugh much anymore," they say.

What should I do with this dead plant? Should I throw it out or cut it back, add some water, dig around and try to find some life worth saving? I determine it is easier to go to buy a nice, new, waxy plant. If the shackles of grief ever free me to laugh again, my laughter will be different. It will go deeper. The laughter and joy will come from one who has been dead.

The pain of grief knocked me out of the dazed state of numbness. The psalmist's lament and prayer for healing from sickness described his pain like arrow wounds: "For your arrows have sunk into me, and your hand has come down on me" (Psalm 38:2). I know this arrow. The arrow pierced my heart, and my heart broke into pieces like a shattered pottery vessel. For the next two years I would be putting the broken pieces of my life back together to yield a new creation. "Why does it take so long?" I would keep asking. Grief shatters who we are and causes us to put our lives back together in a new way. When David the king learned of his son Absalom's death, he "was deeply moved, and went up to the chamber over the gate, and wept; and as he went, he said, 'O my son Absalom, my son, my son Absalom! Would I had died instead of you, O Absalom, my son, my son!' " (2 Samuel 18:33).

Like an arrow falling from the sky, the call came from some unknown transmitter. Sooner or later we all receive such a call. When the call came to me, I could see the black volcanic rock accenting the Oklahoma hills. Buffalo were on the horizon grazing on the new green shoots of grass. I imagined hearing the buffalo pulling up that young grass out of the ground, roots and all. Grazing on the new grass seemed shortsighted to me as I watched them swallow it whole, knowing that they would chew on it later. How could Hannah be plucked up at such a young and tender age, like the young and tender grass that the buffalo greedily eat. What kind of force in the universe would take the lives of children?

While in Phil's office I cried and went to the bathroom to urinate. It seemed that every five minutes I would have to go to the bathroom again. My body was doing strange things in those first agonizing moments of shock. I knew that before death the body gets rid of waste, and I wondered if I were going to die. I called some friends. One friend was in the closet with her children—another tornado was passing over Birmingham. Her husband was en route with other friends to find Kelly. I called them on their car phone, and they assured me they would be there for us. I was glad they were coming. I called some clergy friends from seminary who lived in Nebraska. I happened to have their number in my planner. I cried out to my former roommate, "Why did this happen to us? It is not fair."

The only thing I remember my friend saying was, "Dale, you've got to pull yourself together. You've got some important stuff to do now."

Upon hearing that, something inside of me clicked. I internally changed into a new mode of functioning and a different part of my personality calmly answered, like a child obediently answering a father. "Okay," I said. At that moment, I realized that there were several sides of my psyche, all of which would be utilized to help me endure this tragedy.

Over the next hour, waves of screams would come and go—periods of painful grief that sent me to the floor. Then I would recover and remember to breathe and drink a little water. The dance of wailing seemed almost an art. I felt best when I would begin my deep cries standing up, leaning against a wall or pole, and in my cries would dramatically sink down to the floor. I did not set out to make this a consistent dance, nor did I particularly want anyone to see it, but I repeated it enough times that I wondered if it were a dance. "How silly of me, to be reflecting upon the art of appropriate mourning," I thought. However, physically sinking to the floor seemed an appropriate echo for the sinking feeling inside me. Raw grief is chaos; very little makes sense.

I tried to talk Phil out of flying with me to Alabama, but he would not listen. Deep down, I was relieved, though, because the trip home was nearly unbearable. The hardest time was during a layover in Dallas. Phil was gone perhaps ten minutes to call his mother. Those ten minutes were the longest and most painful. I had no mother to call. I read Psalm 23, but it did not console me. I just panicked. Like Alice in Wonderland, I was falling into a deep, black hole. Just sitting there in the airport terminal, surrounded by people who were trying to be busy, I was coming unglued. I wanted to lie on the floor and groan and scream. "Don't panic," I told myself over and over again. Maybe I could try some breathing exercises. I considered myself a good Lamaze coach when Hannah and Sarah were born, "Blow, breathe, then grit your teeth and blow the 'hee hee' breath." I was desperate to do anything to keep from exploding, but it didn't work. The pain in my stomach bent me over forward. I was falling into the darkness, and nothing could console me. Nothing could fill my emptiness. I was sure that everyone was watching me nervously twitch and sway. It took all my energy just to keep from screaming, "My Hannah is dead. Stop the world—all is meaningless."

There are moments in our lives when our grief is so heavy that we cannot be consoled. Perhaps this was Jeremiah's experience in his lament over Judah:

> My joy is gone, grief is upon me, / my heart is sick.
> . . . .
> Is there no balm in Gilead? / Is there no physician there?
> . . . .
> O that my head were a spring of water, / and my eyes a fountain of tears, / so that I might weep day and night / for the slain of my poor people! (Jeremiah 8:18, 22a; 9:1)

I looked around me. Everything looked absurd, if not stupid—people going places, rules about smoking, my own pocket planner with all my important appointments and engagements. In that moment, it was all trivial. I was surprised and even frightened by the rage that seemed to come out when I looked around me or spoke. I wondered if I would really lash out at the airline attendants who were asking for simple things. My companion returned, but he couldn't have understood my panic, even when I tried to describe it to him. On the plane to Dallas, the instructions to buckle up for safety and about what to do in an emergency seemed insignificant and strange to me.

I said to my soul, be still, and wait . . .
So the darkness shall be the light,
and the stillness the dancing (T. S. Eliot)

All summer long I found myself digging and planting flowers. During the fall, some students helped me plant pansies. I would see a blooming mum, and I had to have it. At Christmas time, I had to purchase a living Christmas tree that we could later plant in the ground. In the mail, Kelly and I received a box of bulbs to plant with a note that during that person's time of grief, it was helpful to plant and wait for new life. Somehow the search going on inside of me, that yearning and digging around for the new Dale and for new life, I was expressing in actual digging and planting. I chose to dig the hole for the Christmas tree myself. I was planting it in the front yard of the Wesley Foundation, close to where another tree had died. The attendant at the nursery said to dig a hole twice as large as the huge bucket the tree was in, deep enough for the soil to be loose underneath, and filled with rich potting soil. I had a very rich compost pile for just such a purpose. I began digging first thing in the morning. I dug and dug. For me, I was digging a grave. As I dug deeper, I had to get down in the grave. It was near the end of the semester, and my students waved as they would go off to take their final exams. I laughed to myself, thinking, "Here I am digging a grave for my grief, and for Hannah, and they may be about to dig their graves by taking their exams." I thought of my life with Hannah, and somehow through my digging I was able to find some peace. There is something about digging in the earth and planting that helps us symbolize externally what we are experiencing internally. Families used to help dig the graves of their family members, and in so doing they touched death. Now we are distant and protected from the dirtiness of the grave. Kelly and I will plant those bulbs and wait for their growth in the spring, and with their growth will be our internal new shoots of life.

For the Goshen United Methodist Church in Piedmont, Alabama, it has been over nine dark months since the tragedy. Months filled with facing shattered dreams, healing splintered bones, rebuilding homes, and for many of us who had to move, months of replacing household items we had lost. It took most of us nine months to develop in the womb, and now we have had over nine months since the tragedy to prepare for our new lives. The reality of pain is sure, but there have also been moments of grace and moments of comfort. These did not take away the pain, but they have made the pain survivable. Recently I asked a member of the congregation who lost her daughter and husband, and who was in the hospital for seventy-three days, if she had good days and bad days. She quickly said, "I have not had any good days." Her honesty reminded me that grief goes deep. She would agree, however, that she has grown in many new areas, and found comfort in her faith.

Many writers speak of grief as the season of winter, when our hearts and souls feel absence. Martin Marty writes that the absence of and longing for the one who has died is filled with only "a wintry frost." Others, such as T. S. Eliot, speak of darkness awaiting light, and stillness awaiting dance. We welcome the poet who has the gift to articulate the seasons of life. It has been over nine months of a frosty dark winter in our souls. In the winter of grief, happy songs of praise are irritating. Sing me a slow and dark lament, and save the happy tune for spring. Pretending to be happy and singing happy songs further separates me from myself. Perhaps it would even hamper my healing.

Standing guard on the edge of my borrowed home is a large hydrangea bush. Growing up in Alabama, we called them snowball bushes. During the summer, this bush displays a spectacular bowl of blooming blue snowballs, stretching four feet high and five feet wide. It is the kind of sight that causes you to look twice. Fall turns the blooms brown, and as winter approaches the leaves follow suit. The bush looks to be dead and dormant, but to my surprise, occasionally, a green shoot appears, complete with about three pea-green leaves and a small blue bloom. These occasional blooms remind me that even in the dark and frosty days of winter absence, new life can come unexpectedly, out of season, to comfort, console, and offer companionship. When you are living in winter, you may not want to hear people say that they made it to spring; but perhaps deep down, you allow the seed to be planted, in hope for a spring thaw. There is no rush, for experiencing the fullness and depth of grief takes patience and time. We spend years creating our worlds, with walls filled with charts of how things will be, and calendars filled with future plans. Now all those internal charts and plans are lying on the floor of our hearts, and our unconscious must begin rebuilding the wall, and rearranging the new person. There is no quick fix, no fast food. Internal work is slow.

On the plane, Phil did most of the talking for me. I assumed he knew I was having trouble communicating, but I doubt he knew how badly I needed him in those moments. I didn't realize it either. He was an angel for me that day: a person of grace, who allowed me to cry, led me around, and calmly took care of me like a father. Phil, in his mid-fifties, is a large man, full of warmth and care. He had been a campus minister at Cameron University for over twenty years. He listened, and somehow his presence gave me assurance that I would be taken care of. I could talk to him; he kept me calm. Someone needed to be in control, and I didn't qualify, for I was filled with rage and gut-wrenching pain. Oh, the rage. Oh, the pain.

From Dallas to Birmingham, our seats were in the back of the plane, and I calmly tried to tell Phil that I wanted to be the first one off the plane in Birmingham. I could not imagine standing and waiting in line. I tried to tell an attendant, but the words would not come. Phil told the attendant that I had lost people in the tornado in Alabama, and I wanted to get off the plane first. She looked at me as if I were an alien requesting the unthinkable and hurriedly left.

Perhaps she saw my rage or felt sorry for me because she could see that I could not stop shaking. Perhaps on earlier flights she had experienced others who had actually exploded when asked to wait their turn in line. Perhaps she had experienced grief herself and knew of the pain that I was feeling. Others on the plane turned and stared as if seeing a freak. Did I look that bad? I was trying so hard to keep the waves of exploding pain inside and not let it show. I thought, "Can they see that my insides have been ripped open today? Perhaps the wounds are showing. Well, they are lucky, because if my pain really was showing, I would be screaming, jumping up and down, and probably hitting people." I smiled at the thought.

Something from the recesses of my mind began to haunt me. It was as though I knew something important but had forgotten it. I closed my eyes and strained to remember. A previous conversation came to mind. The night before, I had visited a powwow at the Apache Community Center. A leader of the Apache tribe told me of the death of her grandchild a few months before. She pointed out her daughter, who appeared to be in her twenties, talking in the crowd. I saw her short hair as she danced. Her youngest daughter looked to be about sixteen. She was the tribal princess this year and danced beside her big sister. She pointed out her son, and her husband at the microphone. All the members of her family had cut their hair after the death. While in the van driving the students home that night, I reflected upon the conversation, and thought to myself, "When I have my tragedy, maybe I will shave off my beard." I repeated what I had thought, "Not *if*, but *when*." Had some part of my inner self known that I would be on this plane going to bury my daughter? I dared not mention my thoughts to Phil.

The attendant returned shortly and said she had found seats for us closer to the front. In fact, she had asked someone to rearrange in first class to make room for us. This special treatment meant the world to me. Phil and I talked of many things. He listened, and I remember he offered only one piece of wisdom: "People usually do the best they know how to do." I had heard and even said this before, but I heard it with new ears, in this situation.

I was surprised at the large crowd at the airport to meet me—some friends, some preachers, my sister and her husband . . . and the bishop. It was only later that I realized how much trouble he had gone through to be there to meet me. He is very sensitive, and the destruction had shattered him, but he was determined to be a pastor and friend to Kelly and me, as well as the church. And here I was, a walking zombie, raw, exposed to my boss.

A friend handed me a folded sheet of paper that partially listed the names of the dead. I glanced down at the list. I felt happiness that some names were not listed, but sadness at seeing the names of others. I felt guilty for my joy that some friends had survived—not because I wished for the others' death, but because my joy somehow seemed to dishonor the dead. Just as I was folding the paper to put it in my pocket, I noticed the name of one of my students: Wes Voorhees. This was too much. I had asked him to sing the solo in the Palm Sunday drama at Goshen, and now because I had asked he was dead. I felt guilt and wondered how I would face his parents. I couldn't bear any more tonight. How much pain can a person take at once? I lived with that heavy burden until the morning, when I learned that Wes was in the hospital, alive.

My sister and her husband drove me to our district superintendent's home, where Kelly and Sarah were staying. My sister, Connie, warned me that Kelly was pretty badly injured. She had suffered a nasty blow to her forehead, had various deep cuts on her legs, and a separated shoulder that needed medical attention. She told me that Kelly was not in a condition to think straight and that I needed to help her get to the doctor. I had a terrific headache and took several Tylenol. We were silent during much of the trip. I realized that it was again time to retrieve some part of myself that could take control and be strong.

I thought of ordinary memories of Hannah, not so ordinary anymore. My last sight of her was as she stood, three feet, six inches tall, wearing a blue dress, waving on the sidewalk outside the church. Before I left, she had run a favorite route up the sidewalk toward the church, and Kelly had stopped her before she completed her customary lap around the church and back to our house. Hannah wrapped her arms around me and said, "Bye-bye, Daddy. I love you." She waved until my car was out of sight. Little scenes flashed before my mind's eye: holding, rocking, and singing her to sleep; the spirited way she was constantly moving, climbing, and asking questions. Perhaps such everyday occurrences had not been so ordinary after all. In grief, we often memorize certain scenarios and play them over and over again in our minds. In *Cold Sassy Tree,* Olive Ann Burns describes this process as what happens when "You realize you are thinking about that person like you are memorizing them or something."

I reminisced about the happy memories of taking Hannah and Sarah to Disney World a few months earlier. I was glad I had begun to take the girls to the beach at Gulf Shores one weekend a month for family time. I remembered how each night I said to my girls, "Have I ever told you that I love you?" Sarah, age two, would just grin.

But Hannah would respond with a giggle, "Oh, Daddy, you tell me that all the time."

A memory flashed: Kelly stood in the carport to tell me goodbye. I could almost read her mind when I saw a familiar look of panic on her face, which said, "Here you go, leaving me for ten days with all this responsibility." With a teasing grin, she leaned over to me and said, "Are you sure you don't want to take one of the children with you?"

My memory turned to a guilty feeling. I asked myself, "Why didn't I even consider it? If only I had . . . " I was trying to gain some control over the uncontrollable. Even claiming responsibility would give me some control; there would be some order in the universe.

My sister told me that lots of people would help us. I was silent. Rage came again with a flash, and I thought, "I don't want to be pitied. I don't want to be helped, I just want Hannah back." Then I thought the opposite, "Somebody had better help us. Somebody had better find us a new home away from Piedmont."

I was beginning the constant struggle of grief, pushing away those around me, and simultaneously expecting them to stay quietly. I felt humiliated having to ask for the simplest things. It is no wonder that people can't stand to be around those who are grieving. We are impossible to comfort. We are selfish and need others to bring us food, to talk and to be quiet, or to make us laugh. We are impossible to please. We want it and don't want it at the same time. We are falling into a well with no control, no brakes. Nothing can console us: no scripture, no meaning, least of all anything logical. Death robs us of all logic and makes jokes of our sure plans.

As we approached the first of several homes that would accommodate us over the next few weeks, I began to panic. "I can't do it," I thought. We pulled into the driveway, and I froze. I was about to face my wife, suffering from the worst loss of our lives, and my knees locked. I felt myself moving my head up and down like an agitated horse, and I was saying, either silently or verbally, "I can't face it." My hands intensely rubbed my thighs—back and forth, back and forth. The car door opened, but I sat like a frozen zombie. I looked at other zombies approaching my car. Some faceless person reached for me, and I got out. Someone gave me a hug. I cried. Oh, how I cried. It was good that I cried outside the house, because I would have been embarrassed inside, for the house was full of people awaiting our return.

As I nervously entered the door, I saw her. The world around us stopped as our eyes met. This was the moment when Kelly and I would share the worst loss of our lives. We slowly glided into each other's arms. As I wrapped my arms around her shoulders, she flinched and said, "Not this side." We had a long, one-sided hug. The familiar expression, "I love you," seemed to be the only offering we could make to each other. I heaved with tears and cries as she embraced me. Then I backed up to look at Kelly. She looked terrible. Before I greeted those waiting to see me, I had to see Sarah. Sarah, my two-year-old angel, was sleeping. I touched her, patted her. Standing there looking at Sarah, Kelly and I cried silent tears. Sarah looked like Hannah once looked while sleeping. I said, "I need just a few minutes to be here with you and Sarah." Kelly's silence conveyed her understanding.

By now, it was after eleven o'clock. Back in the den, we briefly visited with those who had gathered to show their support. We said goodnight and thanked them for coming, and they left to make the long two- to three-hour drive home. I imagined that they would go into their children's rooms when they got home and stand looking at their children, perhaps pat them and give them a kiss, and say an extra prayer of thanksgiving for their lives. The next morning they would be back at our side.

Many people had made great sacrifices to share this moment, however brief. I have often thought how we underestimate our own deep resources of compassion; then an accident, a disaster, a death happens, and we act before we have time to think about what we are doing. In these initial responses humans are capable of great acts of compassion. Usually, we are surprised at our own enthusiasm and generosity. It is similar to falling in love. Something inside us seems to trick us into falling in love with one particular person, and we are in over our heads before we realize what we have done. For years, in my work with students and churches, I have thought that the less we isolate ourselves from those hurting in the world, the more we can foster our own wells of compassion. Our culture discourages us from touching death, illness, and tragedy. This isolation leaves us unprepared for tragedy when it occurs.

What do you do when someone you know is grieving?

To be alert to the needs and wounds of others is to be fully alive. To live with passion and compassion is to be moved by the pain of others. This compassion that moves us toward others is a love that mysteriously brings deep friendship and happiness. For the grieving, the thought of journeying alone can be devastating. Helping the grieving is loving them enough that you do not leave them to their own devices.

Since the tornado, many people have asked me what they should do to respond to those who are grieving. I tell them that it was helpful to us when persons brought food and came by to see us and call. We were not able to see everyone, but each call, note, and visit gave us strength. I got angry when people told me, "Don't worry, it will be okay." But it was helpful when they said, "You are doing great," and "You are stronger than you think." Because grief took away my self-esteem, I needed encouragement. Many people helped us with housekeeping chores we couldn't do. When people asked if they could help, often I didn't want to admit I needed help, or I couldn't think of anything for them to do. But when someone looked around and said, "Let me take your laundry home and bring it back in the morning," that was a specific thing that really was helpful, as was helping clean the house, or answering the phone, or simply writing down the names and addresses of people who brought food and flowers. It is not always helpful to keep a grieving person occupied in conversations. Simply listening and praying for someone who is grieving is helpful. One of the things I regret is that many ministers asked me what they could do, and I wanted them to hold my hand and pray for me, but I was embarrassed to ask. And rarely did they offer. It was God's strength I needed more than anything.

The rain had stopped, and Kelly and I went outside on the patio for privacy. Cold wetness soaked quickly through my pants as I realized I was seated on a wet chair. About that time, Mrs. Williamson was walking through the door, talking about its being wet and cold on the patio. She brought us some towels to wipe off the chairs. This was the beginning of her new role as caretaker of the Clems. As she left, Kelly apologized for my wet pants. I said, "It doesn't matter that I look like I just wet my pants." She laughed and we were refreshed by the humor of the moment. If ever there was a time when having wet pants was insignificant, it was now.

"Are you okay?" Kelly asked. She quickly added, "I know you're not okay, but—"

I interrupted, "Yes, I'm just very confused about what happened."

"It just happened so fast. I don't know why I don't remember more. Maybe the brick that hit my head knocked me out. We were in the middle of the musical drama; the lights went off, and we were trying to go on without the sound system. A window broke. I tried to go for Hannah, and the building exploded. When I raised up, I was outside. All I saw were piles of concrete blocks, beams, broken wood, glass, and dirt. There was a 'chink, chink' sound of bricks moving, and coughing. I was coughing, spitting, trying to get the grit out of my mouth. I was confused and thought, 'Where did the church go? Where did the people go?' Then I realized that people were trapped under three or four feet of rubble."

As she spoke, my body drew up and squirmed as I tried to imagine such a horror.

She continued, "There was an eerie silence. People were not screaming or crying. I tried to get Hannah. I was desperate to find her. I felt so bad, not helping others before I dug her out. Everybody needed help, and I had to choose whom to help first. I did help pull some children out, but I wanted to get to Hannah first. Everywhere I tried to step I was stepping on people. It was more like climbing over rocks than walking. It was terrible. I heard moans under the buried rubble, but I couldn't see who was underneath. We tried so hard to move the blocks off Hannah. It felt like an eternity as we were digging and throwing blocks. I could see a scrap of her blue costume through the blocks, but we just couldn't get to her.

"Amy (a spunky ten-year-old) was hurt very badly. A huge concrete beam was on top of her. Dale, you would not believe how big and heavy it was. Amy was on a pew, and Hannah was under the pew. I think that Hannah had gotten under the pew like she had been taught in preschool." (Hannah was very proud of knowing what to do in case of a tornado and had practiced it several times.) "Before we could get to Hannah, some men had to get that concrete beam moved off of Amy. They carried Amy out using the pew as a stretcher. When we got the blocks off Hannah, I touched her and patted her and told her it would be all right, 'Mommy is here.' But Dale, she was already dead. She was cold and gray. She was just too little. A bigger person might have made it under those blocks, but she was just too little."

During the Christmas season, I have pondered that God must have had anxious moments as a father when Jesus was a vulnerable baby born in such a violent time. Surely God knew the dangers of bringing a child into the world. Surely, parents who find themselves cooing, pleasing, and delighting their children would be no different from God. When Hannah asked to sit in my lap, I moved my papers over so that she would feel secure. When she asked to hear a favorite story or song, I became a singer and storyteller. Surely God the Father would have a special ache of love for His son, which would lead him to make up stories, play silly games, and stop important work so that his child could climb in his lap. Perhaps it was hard for God to watch another father raise his son, hoping and wishing Joseph would not be too tired or busy to sing silly childish songs and make up fabulous stories. Who did God pray to when he wanted Joseph to pick up the tiny Jesus and hold him tight against the cruel world? I wonder if God panicked when Herod started killing the babies. I wonder if God the father nervously sent the angel to warn Joseph to flee to Egypt. Did God stay on tiptoe until they were safe? I wonder if watching this drama of a vulnerable tiny baby growing up would be any more traumatic for God than for us? In Whistling in the Dark, *Fredrick Buechner writes of this Word becoming flesh: "Ultimate mystery is born with a skull you could crush one-handed. Incarnation. It is not tame. It is not touching. It is not beautiful. It is uninhabitable terror. It is unthinkable darkness riven with unbearable light. . . . It is the resurrection and the Life she holds in her arms. It is the bitterness of death he takes at her breast."*

I was relieved at the thought that maybe she didn't suffer. I began to invent reasons why it was okay for her to die. At least she didn't suffer. It is a hard world anyway. Getting over this trauma would have been tough for her. What if she had been brain-damaged? It's better she got to go on and die. She's with God. All these justifications give a momentary peace to help me accept her death. It's strange how these explanations temporarily push away the pain and give us a sense of control. My sense of being out of control as well as my sense of meaninglessness was what was driving me mad. This meaninglessness caused my brain to attempt to make order and meaning—to invent reasons justifying her death.

I felt sorry for poor little Hannah being trapped under such rubble. What would she have thought? A tremendous wave of pity shook my body, and I shivered. I wasn't sure if the wet cold had finally penetrated my skin or if it was indeed the pity that was permeating my inner being. Poor Hannah, she was just too little. I imagined her spirit leaving her body and looking around on its way through a tunnel of light to meet my parents and grandparents. I had heard other people's accounts of near-death experiences. I hoped Hannah's departure was a peaceful one. I imagined all those people's spirits leaving at once from the rubble of the church. But it was hard to visualize, because I hadn't yet seen the rubble.

We had spent so much energy trying to help Hannah have a happy life. We had worked so hard on potty training, keeping her healthy, giving her outlets for her never ending energy. "For what?" I thought, "She is now dead at four. Not a very long life."

"What happened?" had been my constant question for the day. Little did I know that it would become the question that would rule my life for the next year.

What I learned in the months to come helped me put the pieces of the story together. Understanding the tragedy was an essential part of my grief process. I have wondered if it was understanding that led to meaning and acceptance. Hearing what many people remembered helped me get a glimpse of what happened, and that glimpse helped me accept the tragedy.

Elisabeth Kübler-Ross, in writing about death and dying, reports that people, even children, often anticipate their own deaths. There are countless stories of people who, although they did not know exactly when and how they would die, have been aware that they were moving toward the mystery of death.

In her four years and eight months of life, Hannah had asked her share of questions. Sometimes she would follow her mother and me around asking us one question after another; and at other times, she would be playing and climbing on the monkey bars, her favorite playground equipment, and urgently run to us with a new question she had been pondering in her swings, reaches, and jumps. Since both her parents were pastors, she probably had more than her share of church experiences.

In her own spiritual life, I am sure that she had a relationship with God. Her reverence regarding her small *Toddler's Bible* surprised me. We never discussed it, but somehow she decided that her Bible was more important than the other books she loved. She loved the story of Jesus being born in a stable among animals. At Christmas time, she would take the baby Jesus from the crèche and put him in her secret hiding place. She loved the creation story, which in her language says, "God made everything." From an early age, she thought that God was up in the sky. She would ask her mother and me, "Is God way up there in the sky?" We would answer yes. She would respond, "Let's throw this ball up high in the sky, to God." With all her might she would throw the ball as high as she could, only to be disappointed when God did not catch it. God was a friend, a playmate, a companion in Hannah's eyes.

Weeks before Palm Sunday, Kelly came into her room and saw Hannah looking out the window, through the large oak trees that were about to sprout green leaves, and heard

Hannah thanking God for her family. When Kelly entered, Hannah turned with a bashful look on her face. "It's okay, Hannah," Kelly said. "You know you can always talk to God."

"Does God see everything that happens, even when trees fall?" asked Hannah.

"Of course," answered her mother.

"Then does God have fourteen heads?"

Kelly looked puzzled, and she said, "Hmmm, I'll have to think about that one."

Monday, March 28, 1994

A Picture of Heaven

We tried to sleep during the night. Close to morning, Kelly and I realized we were both wide awake and staring at the ceiling. She looked at me and said, "I just had an unusual dream."

Kelly described her dream, "All night long I was lifting bricks, then throwing them out of the way. There were others around me but we kept doing the same activities, over and over again. My whole world seemed gray and dull. The feeling was so hopeless; yet we just kept digging through the rubble, hoping to find human life. Suddenly I was standing away from the scene, and right in the spot where Hannah had been buried under the rubble, I saw children, dressed in beautiful, bright colors. They seemed to be oblivious to the rest of us. They were playing and laughing with each other. The grass they were standing on was bright green. Dale, the colors were such a contrast to the rubble in the sanctuary where we were standing. I just can't get over the color I saw."

Kelly's vision has given her something to hold on to. It has helped me to consider this image of peace in the midst of utter chaos. The children were safe. Kelly was the one seeing the bleak and dismal situation, while the children seemed to be in their own world, free from the gloom around them.

It was this dream, this sign, this vision that gave Kelly a peace not only the next day but also even to this day. Our faith teaches us that there is another world after this one, but we have no proof that it exists. For Kelly, this dream was all the proof she needed: a vision of peace, a sign that Hannah and the others were okay. Those of us here on earth, trying to clean up the mess and reorder our lives and develop new roles, are not okay. Through reading and talking to people about near-death experiences, we learned that as people experience themselves moving out of their bodies, through a tunnel, toward the next life, the colors and light they see are brighter than anything they have seen on earth. In Kelly's mind, what she had seen was a gift from God, one that would see her through many hard days.

In a year of constantly asking what happened, I learned that many people had had similar visions and experiences, which brought them peace and helped bring order and meaning to the utter despair and chaos of death. Not surprisingly, many people are hesitant to share such experiences, because a poem or vision may bring comfort, but if shared, another person could discount the experience and put a damper on what once gave grace and meaning.

Kelly remembered that right after the tornado passed and as she stood up, she looked up to the clear sky and prayed, "Send help!" and immediately men appeared at the side of the sanctuary. Ambulances came. Prayer was answered.

The bishop was at our house early Monday morning. He was dressed in a business suit with a white shirt and a dark, traditional tie. To me, he seemed businesslike in what he expected to accomplish. His order of business was to oversee the pastoral care for the congregation and to accompany us back to the disaster site. When he arrived, we were still trying to develop a list of those who had died and those who were in the hospital. Kelly did not know that I had a partially correct list, and she was surprised to see some of the names. She had seen and known some people were dead, but not others. As she looked at the list, she flinched as she saw a name and said, "They looked really bad," or, "They didn't even look hurt." How odd, I thought, looking at the names of people as if they were items on a grocery list. But I had not experienced what Kelly and this congregation had experienced. After we fed Sarah and the babysitters arrived, we would leave to see the damage. Kelly had agreed to do one interview with a CBS news correspondent.

Visiting the Site

Blue lights flashing were the first things I could see as our car crawled north on Highway 9 toward our house and the church. Twenty-four hours earlier, the parking lot, which extended in a horseshoe shape from each end of the highway and around the church, was filled with cars and trucks for the Palm Sunday service. Tall oak trees, cedar trees, and others shaded the edges of the parking lot. During the tornado, these trees had fallen on many of the cars, and debris from neighboring homes was scattered over the area. Cars had been hurled from one end of the lot to the other and were strewn everywhere. It amazed me to learn that even in the chaos, rescue vehicles were at the church within ten minutes. For two hours following the disaster, emergency lights had flashed up and down Highway 9 and down a narrow path to the victims. Small four-wheel-drive vehicles reached the site by the farm equipment access road behind the church. Everyone who arrived was mobilized to clear debris using chain saws and car jacks, or to help extricate the dead and injured from the rubble. Folks in Piedmont know the value of an assembly line, and they calmly and quickly found a place to serve.

On Monday morning, only the blue flashing lights were the same. The reporters had come early to stake out a spot. We were told that over twenty satellite trucks were used to send the story to the world. There was a feeling of panic and desperation as the reporters moved about in a frenzy, swarming like yellow jackets, encircling anyone who was willing to talk. As cars arrived in the parking lot, the reporters would lean over the hood of the car and squat beside the windows to see who was within. I was surprised when a state trooper cleared a path for our car to park. "How does he know who we are? Why are all these people running and crowding around?" I asked myself. Something must have just happened. I looked out the window to see what had happened and where the reporters were going. But they all seemed to be looking in our car window. I slowly began to realize that it was Kelly they were waiting to see. I remember it like a slow-motion movie—these panicked faces looking in at us. We started to get out of the car, amidst the mud and tree limbs, surrounded by reporters dressed in casual, crumpled-looking clothes, as though they had been there all night, sleeping in their cars. It reminded me of pictures of reporters covering a war zone. It was a cloudy, rainy day, and the reporters had on their weathered raincoats. A reporter asked, "Who are you?" I smiled but didn't answer. Another asked, "Are you the pastor? Can we get a statement?"

Suits

Our rescuers rushed over, wearing nice suits and ties. The bishop and district superintendent took on the role of secret service agents and escorted us through the reporters. Was it possible to be crushed by the press, who pushed in to get a close-up picture and record any word we might whisper? The bishop and district superintendent flanked Kelly on both sides, escorting her toward the house. The reporters pressed in and I found myself pushed back. From this vantage point I noticed the contrast between the ragged look of the reporters, Kelly, and the site itself, and clean, white, starched look of the bishop and the district superintendent. Here we were in a swarm of reporters, in the midst of downed trees, a crumbled church, and the horror of death. Kelly was wearing borrowed, mismatched clothes and size-nine tennis shoes for her size-six feet. She had suffered a hematoma on her forehead, and the skin where the blood had gathered underneath was soft and dark. The reporters were dressed for the rainstorms that continued to loom overhead, and then here were our bishop and district superintendent, wearing suits. Wearing suits was a way in which our leaders had the faith and courage to attempt to gain control over a situation that could not be controlled. In the midst of carnage and devastation, they were trying to say to themselves and the world, "We will survive this." I imagined a man in rags holding his arm high in defiance against the crashing sea. The bishop and district superintendent represented the church and took on the role of survivor. I thought of the scripture that says we are fools for Christ (1 Corinthians 4:10). Perhaps those men wearing suits were not the only ones who looked foolish. There were also those of us who dared to stand in the midst of death and destruction and speak of a loving God. Yet there we stood and still stand. We stand as ones not in control, without great understanding, but daring to believe when nothing makes sense. As I stood looking at those suits and the leaders trying to bring dignity and order to the chaos, a cynical part of myself said, "Just let it go; don't try to bring order and control—there is none."

But what did Kelly and I do through our attempts to be strong and talk about the tragedy? Many called us courageous and heroic. We were really just wearing suits of a different kind from those of the bishop and district superintendent. We were trying to draw order from chaos, hope from despair, compassion from suffering. We too wore suits; they just were not of the same design.

Press Conference

The little mob moved closer to our house. Reporters who had gotten close to Kelly in front and back tried hard not to lose their place. Huge microphones with their fuzzy black covers loomed overhead, threatening to bob Kelly's already badly bruised forehead. I noticed more camera crews and reporters with little tape recorders frantically running to get close. I felt pity for these folks who seemed to be so desperate to get their story. I thought, "Slow down! The world isn't going to end if you don't get a story." Of course, for them, getting a story probably did mean keeping their jobs. Kelly later laughed, thinking about the microphones resembling feather dusters. While the microphones were above her head and under her chin, she wondered if they would try to tickle her.

I had never imagined that anyone really wanted a story from Goshen. We were a small, rural community where nothing ever happens to attract the national or even local news crews. The one exception was our neighbor in Gnatville, whose bird dog shot him while he was hunting last year. The hunter was climbing over a fence and had laid his gun down beside the fence. Somehow the safety latch was pushed off, and the jumping dog landed with his foot right on the trigger. The shot barely hit the hunter's foot. This story made National Public Radio.

Earlier that morning, I welcomed my time in the shower as a time to cry, be alone, and pray. Thoughts and memories kept racing through my mind, but it was what my friend said to me the day before that kept coming back to mind, "You've got to pull yourself together, Dale, you've got stuff you've got to do." The shower was warm. I prayed, "God, Kelly agreed to a TV interview today. What do I have to say?"

I leaned back into the shower and felt the warm water hitting the top of my head. Then it clearly dawned on me. I could tell how Hannah helped me to slow down and notice life. The memory of visiting the Anniston Museum of Natural History just a few weeks before flashed through my mind. Sarah was frightened and closed her eyes as she walked past stuffed elephants, giraffes, and birds. Hannah would describe to Sarah what she was seeing, but Sarah did not want to look. It was only toward the end of our tour that Sarah decided to take a peek at a little model of a pygmy village. She enjoyed looking at that and so, with Hannah guiding Sarah, we went through the entire museum again. Hannah patiently showed Sarah her favorite parts—the dinosaur, the elephant, the bees, the birds. Hannah reveled in her visit to the museum.

It was getting late, but Hannah wanted to go along the trail through the woods to "wake the owls." The museum was in the process of placing different owls in tall cages along a trail that looped behind the museum. I could see the loop and was in a hurry to accomplish our task—walk along, see the owls, and be finished with the museum. As the sun began to set, the air was cooling. Hannah's adventure, however, had just begun. Hannah had on jeans with seven pockets, which she filled with little rocks and leaves and twigs. When she had no room left in her pockets, she began to give away her newly found treasures. Each artifact was a source of wonder and amazement to her four-year-old eyes and heart. She and Sarah kept venturing off the trail through the thin pine forest, playing on a felled tree or bringing rocks to me for safekeeping. Hannah acted as though they were the greatest rocks she had ever seen. Both she and Sarah enjoyed picking up sticks and dragging them through the leaves or dirt. The desire to tap trees and rocks with sticks must be a primal instinct. I was impatient and wanted to finish the small loop trail, but for Hannah and Sarah the woods were full of things to see; and Hannah enjoyed everything she saw. Finally, I caught a glimpse of the woods through Hannah's eyes, and I asked myself, "Dale, why were you trying to finish the task of the hike, when our time together was really about looking and seeing and loving?" I thought of Sarah going through the museum with her eyes closed, missing out on the great mysteries of life. I realized that it was I who was walking with blinders, missing the sights and mysteries my children were seeing and enjoying. When did I forget how to scream with joy? Perhaps when I was their age, I too knew that release.

The mob was still moving, and I moved with it, listening to the questions. "Reverend Clem," one addressed Kelly, "we understood that after you knew of your own daughter's death, you continued to help and pray with people." I was surprised at the reporter's question. How did they know something I didn't know? "Reverend Clem, what gave you the strength to go on and minister when you were suffering so much yourself?" And yet another asked, "Reverend Clem, I understand that someone in your congregation asked why this had happened, and you said, 'Now's not the time to ask why, but we just need to help one another.'" Kelly was affirming that these things were true. I was wondering where these reporters learned these stories. I was involved in the situation, and the reporters knew more of what had happened than I did. Members of the congregation had told the reporters about Kelly's behavior during the rescue effort.

Kelly answered a reporter, "Yes, someone screamed, 'Why, Kelly? Why did this happen?' and I think I said, 'Now is not the time to ask why, we just need to help one another!'" The headline in *USA Today* for Monday, March 28, read, "Day of Prayer Turns to Terror: Ala. Church Can Only Ask Why?" Other stories reflected this same question. It was this bewildering question that I saw in the eyes of the reporters leaning over our car.

The mob fanned out a little, giving room for a makeshift press conference. The bishop was telling the reporters that we would answer some questions. Kelly was scanning the crowd. When our eyes met, I realized she had been looking for me. She motioned for me to come and stand at her side. I don't know if the bishop whispered it to us, or where I heard it, but I heard someone say, "The press think that God did this, and they keep asking about it." We stood in front of our front porch, where lay a broken Easter tree whose colored plastic eggs were scattered over the porch and yard. I stood next to Kelly, and I think we held hands. The bishop stood on one side and the district superintendent stood on the other. Kelly described what she remembered, and told about Hannah's being prepared for tornadoes at her preschool. A reporter asked the question I had been wanting answered, "Did you not know a tornado was coming?"

"No, had we been warned, we would not have had church," Kelly answered. Then her trailing voice reiterated, "We were never warned."

The press asked, "Why would God allow this kind of thing to happen to a church?"

I responded by saying that it is never God's will for children to die in disasters. Our God is a God of love. A tornado is an act of nature.

A reporter asked, "What have you learned?"

This was a question I had prepared for. I told them that Hannah had taught me much about life, and that I suspected she would teach me much in her death. The puzzled reporter asked for clarification, and I told them about seeing the world through Hannah's eyes, referring to our hike together at the museum.

A reporter asked, "What do you think you will learn from her death?"

I responded, "I'll have to let you know on that."

A reporter asked Kelly, "This has really shaken us up in our faith. Isn't this tragedy going to shatter your faith?"

Kelly calmly responded, "It hasn't shattered my faith. I am holding on to my faith. My faith is holding me. All of the people of Goshen are holding on to each other, along with the hope that they will be able to rebuild. Easter is coming."

After the interview Kelly turned and saw the fallen Easter egg tree our friend had made for Hannah and Sarah. The cameras were rolling, and we all watched her dramatically stand the tree upright, with its brightly colored ribbons and eggs, and some empty ribbons where eggs once hung. Through her tears, Kelly pressed the tree into the pot of dirt as deeply as she could, as if saying, "This is not going to destroy us." She turned and as she was stepping down said through her tears, "That was Hannah's tree." That simple act of resistance was more powerful than anything we had said.

Over the next few days we were constantly asked about our faith, and about the role God played in the tornado. We were interested in discussing the role God was playing in keeping us going.

"Why did your daughter die?" a reporter asked me.

The answer seemed obvious to me. I answered directly, "She was crushed under a wall."

"But why?" the reporter insisted.

"Because a tornado hit the church, and the wall fell on people. If a wall fell on you, you might die too," I said.

The reporter went on, "But why did the tornado hit the church, while the congregation was worshiping?"

"Well," I said, "I think the tornado moved in a straight line, and also hit that tree over there, and that house, and all kinds of things. I don't think the tornado cared. It is simply an act of wind."

The reporter insisted, "Don't you think it was an act of God?"

My mind flashed to the sermon a Baptist minister in Piedmont had preached against women ministers when we moved to town: "The Devil in Our Midst." It was dawning on me that these reporters were going to have a story, and I did not want them to get it from someone who would say that the tornado hit the church because Kelly was their pastor. The church did not deserve that, nor did Kelly. It was at that point that I began to make a conscious effort to cooperate with the press. I would try to articulate my faith as best I could and pray not to embarrass myself or the church. "Just be honest," I thought to myself—"tell what you believe, and if people disagree and attack you, at least you will have your integrity."

I addressed his question, "I don't believe that God caused the tornado to hit the church. God doesn't decide who will suffer and who will not. It is never God's will for children to suffer and be killed so young. God is a loving God. A tornado caused my daughter's death, not God. It was a disaster. We have them all the time in our world—tornadoes, floods, hurricanes, droughts, and earthquakes. We live in a natural world."

The reporter was frantically writing this down, but shaking his head in disbelief. "But this," the reporter continued, "is the church. You'd think you should be safe in the church."

"Why?" I asked. Later when I read Psalm 42, the scene of the reporters came to mind. The psalmist writes that in the midst of deep grief, when "tears have been my food day and night," it is the memory of celebrating festivals in the house of God that sustains him; but he is only tormented and taunted by the question, "Where is your God?" which his adversaries continually press upon him (Psalm 42:3, 4, 10).

Other friends were looking around the site of our house and church. Some ministers were trying to figure out what to salvage from the church wreckage. I was surprised to see some people I recognized. A friend from Birmingham came into our house asking if she could help. "Do you know anything about rabbits?" I asked her.

She said, "No, but I can learn."

"Great" I replied. "Hannah's pet rabbit Benjamin is on the porch in a box."

She took care of the rabbit for months.

Other friends asked if they could help, and I said, "Well, my fish are going to die without electricity to run the filter system; can you take the fish?" They started the process of moving our aquarium to their home.

I was overwhelmed by the press, but fortunately they seemed to respect our personal boundaries by not asking to come inside our home. The press reminded me of the biblical character Ishmael. Ishmael found himself at odds with everyone.

On Sunday afternoon, while Kelly was at the hospital, ministers had found our house unlocked and begun to see if they could protect our belongings from the rain and weather. They knew that the roof was off one end of the house and were surprised to find that the ceiling had not yet completely fallen in our spare bedroom. We used this bedroom mainly for storage, and it was full. The water was pouring in, so they began to move furniture, books, clothes, and boxes to the living room and den. At the same time, people were bringing over to our den and carport things they thought could be salvaged from the church. It didn't take long for our living room and den to become full, leaving only small aisles to navigate.

Looking at the mess, Kelly said to me, " The house looked so clean this weekend!" I wanted to have a moment away from the people inside and outside our home, so I went to our bedroom. I had not wanted to cry in public because I could envision my sobbing being replayed on the news over and over again like the footage of Rodney King's beating. I went to the bedroom. As I looked out through the broken window, I saw a telephoto lens on a camera, with a reporter snapping pictures. I said, "Oh . . . I can't even find a place to cry." I laughed and went back in with the other people, not knowing what to do. I noticed that Kelly was back outside talking to reporters. I thought, "Why is she going outside and talking to them?" I went out and listened and thought, "Who is this person who keeps talking to the reporters?"

Kelly said that answering questions about what happened was part of her grief process. The national press were very insistent, even though compassionate, in wanting us to do more news interviews and morning news shows. As a person who watches TV, I found it hard to imagine that ordinary people like us would enter the TV world. What I learned was that the world of TV news is full of ordinary folks like us, but that a mysterious distance is placed between the viewer and those in the news.

In thinking about that morning, Kelly said, "The media buffered me from the reality of the scene. It was too hard to go back and face what had happened, but with the media around, it gave me a role, and helped us to get through the pain of going back."

As she walked around that day, Kelly was clutching Hannah's bright pink stuffed kitten. Hannah had gotten this mother kitten for Christmas, along with three small baby kittens that, by miracle of Velcro, fit nicely into the mother kitten's tummy. Hannah loved to line the kittens up and in her high falsetto voice call out, "Mama, Mama, Mama." She would then take the mother cat to find the kittens. Hannah was fascinated by the baby kittens' returning to their mother's womb. She was at the age where she would independently wander away and play for a few minutes, but would come back regularly for a hug, to ask a question, and just check in. Hannah could not check in anymore. Kelly clutched that mama cat tightly. When I asked her why, Kelly just said, "Hannah loved this cat, and seeing it just broke my heart. I just had to hold it." Of all Hannah's toys, it was interesting that Kelly was drawn to the mama kitten. Who would play with this stuffed animal now? Somehow touching Hannah's things seemed sacred. Hugging Hannah's stuffed animals was a way of hugging Hannah. All we had left now were Hannah's things. Is it possible to keep her alive through her toys and memories?

I said, "I just wish some moving and clean-up company could come in here and take our stuff, clean it up, and bring it back to wherever we live." A local minister began calling different moving firms. I thought my idea sounded sane. We would live to regret it over and over again, because it took five months to retrieve all our belongings.

The Red Wheelbarrow

I clambered through the downed trees in my backyard and stumbled upon my little red wheelbarrow. The Friday before I left, I had placed the little wheelbarrow next to our storage building. The storage building was packed full of heavy tools, bicycles, lawnmowers, baby furniture, and Christmas things. The tornado had lifted the storage building and shifted it clockwise about two feet. Our backyard had been fenced in, but there were no fences left standing. The metal was twisted and buried underneath the huge trees now lying on the ground. In the midst of the trees was a child's bicycle, splintered lumber, roofing shingles, pink insulation, metal strips, and other trash. I never found where the bicycle came from.

Our canoe was gone, as well as our camper and the children's playground equipment. Everything in the backyard was a disaster. The legs of our metal garden table were left standing, but the tabletop had flown away. I laughed to myself thinking about the sight of the round metal tabletop flying through the air like a large Frisbee.

In the midst of this wreckage sat the little red wheelbarrow—exactly where I had left it, totally unaffected. It was deep, triangle-shaped, and sat low to the ground on twelve-inch wheels. I had to go and just touch it and move it around.

It was ready for use. I had most recently used it to move fallen limbs from the trees in our yard. Now the trees themselves needed to be moved. This little wheelbarrow couldn't move those things. The most common use it had in our yard was giving the children rides. Hannah and Sarah would sit in the wheelbarrow for long rides around the yard and house. It seemed to be more fun than the wagon.

To me, that little red wheelbarrow represented endurance. It had survived the winds and chaos and was ready to scoop up and carry. The little red wheelbarrow became a symbol of faith. It endured, and it would now scoop us up and carry us around trying to clean up the mess and put our lives back into order. How do we explain the power that faith can play in our lives?

In the days to come, strangers clearing the debris would use this little wheelbarrow to carry loads of limbs, trash, and leaves. I had to grin as I watched. All week long people used it to clean up our yard and the churchyard.

In the weeks and months to come, I would often think about how that little red wheelbarrow survived and how it was ready to help clean up. It is strange to give an object a personality, but somehow, this tool and I have been friends since I was a small boy, and my grandparents used it in their yard. It served them well, and then after their deaths, it became mine. Now it symbolized faith—our faith that endured the storm and our faith that will carry us through the dark days to come.

The Community

There was great power in knowing that people who had suffered losses could relate to others who had also lost possessions and loved ones. It was a mystery to me how such a strong bond developed between those who had experienced the tragedy of Palm Sunday. As an outsider, I just kept trying to get on the inside by asking more questions. Each time I saw a person from the church, I asked questions, trying to put the puzzle together.

During Holy Week, we felt isolated from our community at Goshen. Each family was busy taking care of its own family needs, funeral arrangements, and damaged homes. We could not reach out to one another when we needed one another the most. I wanted to find our friends and give them hugs and cry together, but I just felt lost.

The phone at the home where we were staying did not stop ringing. We had piles of messages from people wishing us love and reporters who wanted interviews. One surprising thing was the number of people who called with prophecies and visions that God had given them. The people who answered the phone and took messages were helpful and patient as these people from around the country called.

On Monday night Kelly and I were exhausted and had slept very little the night before. We finally slept, knowing that we had to get up around four o'clock in the morning to let the camera crews in the living room to set up for the next morning's live broadcasts. As I went to bed, I prayed that God would help us rest and give us the strength to face the coming day.

Tuesday, March 29, 1994

Broken Vessels

"Only you would wake up thinking about Moltmann," Kelly said as she laughed. I was still thinking about the fact that God suffers with us as I showered. I tilted back so the hot water could massage the top of my head. With my eyes closed, I could see the cover of Moltmann's book, with its red and white cross on a black background: *The Crucified God*. This book had been a friend and comfort after the death of my father ten years earlier. Comfort as well as suffering is a mystery to me. However, when I am suffering, I find comfort in the knowledge that God understands suffering.

In just a few days, a *Birmingham News* editorial cartoonist would draw a Good Friday cartoon that connected this suffering God with the Goshen United Methodist Church. He drew the Goshen sanctuary filled with rubble and a fallen cross, and a workman near a bulldozer. With his hat in his hands the workman looks at the rubble and says, "God knows what it was like to be in here." Another workman, looking at the cross, says, "Yes . . . He certainly does."

It was when the Israelites were nearing the end of their exile that the author of Isaiah 53 offered the amazing insight that one's suffering can bring healing to others. The Jews had suffered greatly,

and now the time for gentleness had come. But because of their suffering, they would be a light to other nations. The insight that one could suffer and give life to others helped the early Christians understand the crucifixion of Jesus. In my experience, suffering teaches us on many levels. On one hand, encountering death and suffering shakes me up and helps me regain my priorities in life. Working with the homeless and hungry around the world haunts me enough to help me realize my responsibilities to live more simply and not in isolation. In my own grief and suffering the stories of others helped me heal and know that I was not alone. Their words were like cool water to a dry and parched soul and expressed the feelings I could not articulate. We were amazed at how others who were suffering heard our story and in a mysterious way, hearing this story helped them move through their own grief.

The author of 2 Corinthians 4:7-10 takes this understanding to a new level, writing that we cannot know the suffering God until we ourselves are faced with suffering. It is through our brokenness that Christ's light can shine and bring healing and wholeness to others.

> But we have this treasure in clay jars, so that it may be made clear that this extraordinary power belongs to God and does not come from us. We are afflicted in every way, but not crushed; perplexed, but not driven to despair; persecuted, but not forsaken; struck down, but not destroyed; always carrying in the body the death of Jesus, so that the life of Jesus may also be made visible in our bodies.
> (2 Corinthians 4:7-10)

My life is a cracked clay jar, a broken vessel. The God we seek is the God who is within us, yet we must break the vessel to find the treasure within. In order to know the God who suffers within us, our own vessels must be broken: that is, our lives, our bodies, our spirits. Even though we are ordinary clay jars, we hold within us the light of Christ. The way Christ shines through us is through our cracks, those broken places. Before I had experienced the healing that has come as I have suffered, I thought the idea that suffering *could bring healing to the world was very strange. Yet my experience of sharing common human suffering has convinced me of its truth.*

As the water rinsed away the shampoo, I wondered what my life would be like without Hannah. I knew the grief of losing both of my parents, but not the grief of losing a child. I thought of a lament I wrote after our miscarriage three and a half years earlier. I couldn't imagine the pain of writing another lament. I thought of Rainer Maria Rilke's line, "The greatest gift you have to give the world, is your deepest burden." This burden is a public burden. So many have hidden burdens they can never share. "Do I want anything good to come out of this?" I wondered. Would it lessen or gloss over the depth of pain, or would it bring redemption? I thought, "I'm desperate for some redemption."

Perhaps some redemption would bring meaning to the chaos. Advice I had given to students came to mind, "It is not what happens to you that is important, but what you do about it."

"Damn," I thought. "That is really cruel advice to give to someone who is suffering." It is like adding a burden to the overburdened. Not only am I supposed to deal with the grief, but also I must bear the responsibility of making something positive come out of it. While a part of me was at least ready to talk about something good coming from the pain, another voice kept saying, "Are you sure you are not glossing over the pain?"

Some of the most formative experiences in my life have been when I have touched the wounds of the suffering. Helping clean up and rebuild after Hurricane Hugo and simply listening to the poor in Mexico and Birmingham helped me to understand the connections between human beings. I also was aware of the different worlds that people can inhabit within a mile of one another. You would not have to dig far into my family roots to find poor tenant farmers who lived off the land and tried to raise cotton in exchange for necessities of flour, sugar, shoes, and clothes. My mother wanted me to see and meet the poor in our family who lived in what would today would be considered shacks. She wanted me to appreciate their dedication to hard work, zest for life, and connection to nature. In my ministry, I have tried hard to help people come into contact with those who are suffering and oppressed—visiting with and feeding the homeless, the poor, the hungry. I believe it is through these experiences that we learn about the possibilities of the human spirit. Without these experiences, our deep wells of inner compassion might go untapped. Sometimes it takes a tragedy to shake us out of our complacency and reach out to others. Jesus told Thomas that if he wanted to know him, to touch his hand, his wounded hand. It is a mystery to me that we shrink so much from touching the wounds of others, and yet healing comes from sharing our wounds with others.

"Why not?" was the final reason Kelly and I reached when asked to appear on two live morning news shows. Perhaps God could use us to spread a message of love and empathy for all who are suffering. I wondered if this interview would flesh out Rilke's idea of the gift of sharing our deepest burdens.

At 4:30 A.M., the TV crews arrived. The house was very quiet. I was surprised and touched by the kindness and compassion shown to us by the NBC and CBS news crews. The two networks were able to share equipment and the satellite truck in order to interrupt our lives as little as possible. In this controlled environment, only compassion showed in their eyes—the desperation of the day before was gone.

Kelly and I sat side by side looking at a camera three feet away. Our earpieces kept falling out of our ears and made us nervous about potential technical glitches. We were in shock, we were nervous, and I wondered if my nerves would make my silly smile attempt to hide or deny my pain. If I did smile, would I be disrespectful to the dead?

CBS This Morning was first. At one point Paula Zahn asked, "How severely has your faith been tested?"

I answered, "I expect the days are looking ahead for my faith to be tested. But we are people of faith. I really believe that this is not God's will. God's will is for there never to be suffering and pain. Our suffering and pain is not different from anybody else's around the world. There are people in pain and grief all the time. . . . This morning I woke up thinking about a theologian, Jürgen Moltmann—and Moltmann talks about suffering and the suffering of God—and I started thinking, 'Well, I know we are crying a lot, and I know God is crying too,' and that adds meaning to my life."

The Today Show interview was different. Kelly shared that recently Hannah had talked about death and what happens when you die. Kelly was sure that in Hannah's mind, she knew that when you die, your body is buried, and your heart goes to heaven with God. She had asked if you ever came back, and she had asked her mommy what heaven was like. Kelly said that it is like the most favorite place in the world. Hannah asked if it was like Disney World. Kelly told her yes, it was probably like Disney World.

Katie Couric expressed her surprise that a four-year-old would have talked about death. We could offer no reasons except that she had been around death, and she freely asked questions constantly.

Katie asked me what I had learned from this, and I recounted that I learned to see the world differently, through the eyes of children, similar to what I had said to the press the day before. I think I quoted Rilke's line I had been thinking of earlier: "The greatest gift you have to give the world, is your deepest burden." I explained that we were searching for ways we could now reach out with our burdens.

The interviews were over. I took off my sweat-soaked shirt and put on work clothes. Today we would begin packing our household goods and then meet with friends at the funeral home in the evening. It would prove to be an exhausting day.

Tuesday Morning in Goshen

The front yard of the church looked like a field hospital. The grounds were scattered with bloody towels and quilts, IV tubes, bloody bandages, rubber gloves, children's chairs, torn and shredded spring clothes, broken concrete blocks, reddish-brown bricks, crushed eye glasses, stained sheets, hymnals, and Sunday shoes. Without the crowd of press and satellite TV trucks I got my first glimpse of what it must have been like on Palm Sunday. The sight left me stunned. I wondered if it was somehow sacrilegious just being there. The concrete floor of our carport was stained with blood. Looking down, I thought I would throw up. I knew that it had been used as a temporary morgue before bodies were taken to the National Guard Armory in Piedmont, but I was horrified at the thought of mangled bodies. It is one thing to see a dead body and quite another to see a bloody, injured body. I had missed this part of the story and tried to imagine it, but I couldn't.

These sights must have been here the day before, but I missed them. Perhaps it was the crowds of reporters, or perhaps the shock had kept me from seeing. It gave me an eerie feeling just walking where people had been treated in the triage area and seeing the medical waste lying wet in the grass. Somehow the land cried out to be treated with respect—for on this spot, lives were saved and lives were lost. It was so private I felt guilty for seeing it, like accidentally walking in on your parents making love (or in my case, wondering if they were making love behind closed doors).

This was the same yard where after church on Sundays the children would run in circles. Members would stand around visiting and making plans for lunch or a fishing trip. After church, some members, like Buddy, a young textile worker, fisherman, and weekend athlete, would stand just off the sidewalk in the grass and smoke a cigarette while children gathered around waiting for their questions and kidding. More than once I watched Buddy throw down his cigarette, step on it, and chase children to tickle them. Hannah and other children somehow knew they could play with their friend Buddy. I wondered where Buddy had been stretched out on this triage field before he died. I wondered if the bloody bandage I saw had been used on him. He would have liked being laid in the place where he played with the children. When his own sister had started an IV on him, another sister asked, "Is that Buddy?" The first sister looked closely and realized that she was starting an IV on her own brother; until that moment she had not recognized him because of his injuries and swelling.

A little wooden bench my grandfather Clem had bought from a railroad station was sitting alone on a sidewalk near the church. My brother-in-law had restored it completely. It normally sat under our carport. Someone must have moved it up near the church to provide a seat for the weary. I later learned that Keith Word sat on it while he was waiting for his wife to be rescued from under the roof. Only after his wife had been rescued did he take the ambulance ride to the hospital. Sitting on that little bench, Debra saw the rescue workers carry away the lifeless body of her boyfriend David. As she watched her boyfriend go by, she tried to run to him but was held down by four people. She later learned that only one friend had a hand on her shoulder. She thinks that three angels kept her from running to his body.

The bench was not hurt in the tornado and looked out of place amid the debris scattered around it. I was glad it had been used, but I asked for it to be brought back home. It was time to clean up.

My Wesley Foundation students, now back from Oklahoma, drove the church van in the driveway, pulling the familiar U-Haul trailer. With black garbage bags, gloves, and rakes they began picking up all the medical waste and debris from the front yard. Other students helped our friends and family who were helping clean up and pack the house. A whole freezer full of food was being thrown away, and the refrigerator was cleaned out. Glass was everywhere. People were emptying drawers into boxes and labeling the boxes with encouraging statements like, "You are loved!" and, "The Clems are loved," along with a description of the contents. It was funny to read the statements together: "Bathroom shelf, you are loved." "Dale's underwear, you are special."

I told Kelly I did not want to do any more interviews. But after Kelly had done a few, she introduced me to some nice men doing a United Methodist TV special. She said, "Oh please, this is for the church."

I spoke with all the energy I could, but my words were quiet.

When I saw the TV show, *Winds of Terror, Spirit of Hope*, I realized how exhausted I must have been that day. CNN wanted to tape an interview in our home. It was cold and the interview took too long. With the film rolling, a reporter saw my seven-year-old niece with a sad look on her face, and she asked her what it was like losing her cousin Hannah. Amy burst into tears and ran behind her mother. My sister tried to keep reporters away from her children after that, but her teenage son Kevin's face appeared in newspapers around the world and even in an encyclopedia yearbook. The picture showed him kneeling in the debris of the church with his head in his hands.

From the rubble of the church and churchyard the students gathered a pile of scratched-up shoes. There were children's shoes, men's shoes, and women's dress shoes. There were some men's house slippers. I wondered who wore those to church. A solitary tennis shoe. Another pile was made for sheets, quilts, and towels. I recognized some stained linens that came from our house. They once covered me at night, but now all I could think was, "I want that out of here." It looked as though concrete blocks were arranged in rows in some kind of order across the yard. It meant nothing to me then, but I later found out that many people sat on the blocks holding IV tubes for the injured. Some hymnals were even used as pillows.

I watched a child's Easter hat slowly blow across the yard. I tried to imagine what the yard must have been like when it was filled with my injured friends. The photos in the paper showed such narrow shots, not the bigger picture of 146 injured people and all the helpers. The students made a pile for Bibles, purses, and purple crosses. A young law student was raking and sorting piles of belongings. She looked up and took a breath, letting her rake handle fall to the ground. She grabbed her mouth. If she threw up, I wouldn't blame her. She walked around, and soon was back, raking up jewelry, medical waste, and debris.

Three cereal bowls still sat on the kitchen table with the remains of Sunday breakfast. I discovered them when I lifted up the bathroom door, which had blown off its hinges and rested on the kitchen table. This would have been the last meal Kelly and Sarah ever had with Hannah. The bowls still held the remains of uneaten cereal and milk. It gave me a sickening feeling to see those three bowls. I knew I should move them and clean off the table. But I just stood there imagining the last meal they must have had. Kelly was probably rushing them through breakfast in order to be over at church by the nine-o'clock rehearsal for the special drama. Finally, I just turned and walked out of the room. Why were such ordinary things as stuffed animals, drawings, and cereal bowls becoming so sacred? Again, there was an eerie feeling of witnessing "the last breakfast." I wonder if Leonardo da Vinci's inspiration for his famous painting *The Last Supper* came from his seeing the remnants of a last meal before death.

I have always found holy relics an odd part of the Christian faith. Visiting cathedrals and seeing a bone or a lock of hair of a saint once seemed to me a little sick. But today, everything of Hannah's has become sacred. Why? Surely this is not all we have left. The pain of grief overcame my body, bringing me out of the fog of grief, and sending me to a doorless bathroom cluttered with glass and dirt.

The next time I came into the kitchen, the cereal bowls were cleaned up. "We've just got to move on," I thought. I am glad someone knew just to move on. There is a strange tension between holding on to a loved one and remembering her, cherishing her, and moving on. The necessity of moving on is the saddest part. But I didn't understand that then. Someone else had to move those cereal bowls.

For Kelly, the hardest thing was to take the sheets out of the washer. On Sunday morning before church, Kelly had taken the sheets off Hannah's bed because Hannah had thrown up during the night. Kelly kept remembering the sheets, but she didn't want to touch them. Who would take the sheets and dry them? Someone volunteered; it was done.

Volunteers kept coming. I don't think anyone had asked them to come. They just showed up, hoping to help. Some were old friends; some were new friends. Some people just know what to do and how to help, while others are unable. Experience with death and tragedy may give you the confidence just to "get to work." Many people asked us what they should do for the community and for church members. Kelly later said to me, "Why do they think I should tell them what to do? Can't they go read a book on tragedy and counseling and figure out a plan, then ask my opinion?"

The State Troopers kept a constant vigil beginning on Palm Sunday afternoon. We were told that they would be on our property and protect the area until noon on Wednesday. This gave us one day to clear out our house. However, they stayed constantly during the day for over a week. There were two to four state trooper vehicles lined up in the church parking lot during the day. Their quiet presence gave us confidence to move around freely. Television crews all came and went, filming stories for the nightly news. At one point, four state troopers were standing between their cars, watching while my college roommate and three others were attempting to carry the very heavy wooden altar out of the church sanctuary and load it onto a small pickup truck. As the officers watched, my friend yelled through his straining, "Is this a good show for you?" When the altar lowered the back of the truck, one of the troopers called back, "That's one heavy piece of wood."

Kelly and I walked through the rubble of the sanctuary. I could see only two pews that were not in shreds. Someone had made a clearing near the original center aisle, with the roof on the north side and piles of concrete blocks to the south. The roof of the sanctuary was elevated about four feet by stacks of concrete blocks. Kelly looked at it and said, "Surely the roof wasn't like this on Sunday." I tried to imagine what it would be like with the roof on the ground with its ceiling tiles and metal strips on top of people trapped below.

Kelly showed me the big concrete beams that she tried desperately to lift off Amy and Hannah. I hesitated, but I just had to try to move it myself. I couldn't budge it. Perhaps, if I had been there, maybe I could have moved that concrete beam. I couldn't imagine what having such a weight on me would feel like. How helpless they must have been, like an animal with its foot caught in a trap.

Scattered around in the bricks and blocks were pieces of twisted metal that once framed the windows. Pieces of broken wood paneling were everywhere. "I never noticed so much paneling had been in the church," I thought. Kelly picked up a torn black shoe and said it was hers. She threw it back down quickly. Then she stopped looking, afraid of finding one of Hannah's shoes left behind. Church members combed the rubble looking for their purple crosses, their Bibles, or some jewelry. One half of the sanctuary was still protected by the roof propped up on concrete blocks. Many of us knelt down at the edge of the roof, wondering what was hiding in the blocks and bricks beneath it. I picked up a flattened microphone and wondered what story it could tell.

The Rustic Wooden Cross

Kelly's brother Jeffrey, brought out a wooden cross from one of the offices. He and several church members stood it in several concrete blocks toward the entrance of the sanctuary. You could see it through the open front doors of the church and sanctuary. People brought flowers, laying them at the front steps and at the foot of the cross. Cars crawled by on Highway 9, slowing to look, and often stopping. Sometimes they pulled into the parking lot and got out. The area was roped off by a plastic yellow "caution" tape, but it didn't stop people from coming for a closer look. It didn't take long before someone placed a flowing, bright green philodendron at the foot of the cross. Photographers couldn't resist the opportunity. The cross had already been precious to this church, and it was now the most photographed part of the church. On that day, the cross symbolized the faith that endured in the church even after the tornado. Months later, Kelly would use a text from Habakkuk at Thanksgiving:

> Though the fig tree does not blossom,
>   and no fruit is on the vines;
> though the produce of the olive fails,
>   and the fields yield no food;

> though the flock is cut off from the fold
> and there is no herd in the stalls,
> yet I will rejoice in the LORD;
> I will exult in the God of my salvation.
> (Habakkuk 3:17-18)

The cross symbolized for us the "and yet" of our faith. It meant, as Kelly told the reporters, "We are still the church! The church is not the building, but the church is the people." It offered the appropriate sacred sign to mark the spot where people suffered and died practicing their faith. The wooden cross was made to hang in the sanctuary for the Lenten season a few years before by a much-loved man who had recently died of cancer. With his gentle, loving hands he had made that rustic cross, because Kelly wanted a rugged-looking cross during Lent rather than the regular shiny brass one. Kirk Scroggin, who was playing Jesus in the drama, was to carry it down the aisle and use it to act out the crucifixion, death, and resurrection. Kirk died before he got to carry that cross in the performance. It stood there in the same place for several months. Over time, the flowers died and were left lying limp. The rubble of the sanctuary became a holy altar, and the cross, the focus.

There were risks of injuries as long as the rubble remained, so on a Saturday several months after Palm Sunday, it was decided to burn the rubble and then eventually bury or carry off the remains. I had already decided that I would retrieve the cross from the sanctuary before the fire, but when I got to the church, it was already burning. I went into my house and wept. Reporters asked what it meant to watch it burn, and I had no words to describe my feelings. One feeling was anger at the church members who had started the fire without retrieving the cross from the sanctuary. The heat was so intense we had to stand fifty yards away.

A cat screamed and ran around the burning building. She darted inside and quickly returned, licking her feet. I felt terrible. What would interest this cat in the church except some kittens?

Her screams and mournful cries for her young were heard above the noise of the fire. Something within exploded with a loud boom. That noise and the forceful roar of the flames intensified the screaming of the cat. She, like so many of us, had sought the sanctuary for shelter and safety, and it had turned out to be a place of death. Those standing did not scream outwardly. Tears ran down people's faces, but the cat screamed for us all.

The next day, I looked in the ashes and saw that a layer of gray and black soot covered the concrete floor and blocks. Black nails were everywhere. I didn't look for the cross. But the following day, a friend came to visit, and I showed him the place where Hannah was killed. We walked around carefully on the soot and through the piles of bricks and cement blocks, avoiding the nails. There was a place where rubble was cleared and the soot was thin. There in this place lay the wooden cross. I shouted and ran and picked up the sentimental cross. It looked as if it had no markings of the fire. Chill bumps ran across my body. I wondered if I had witnessed a miracle. I picked up the cross and carried it on my shoulder. How could it be? I asked several people if they had taken it out of the church and then put it back after the fire. No one seems to know how it managed to land on the clear spot in the sanctuary and survive the fire. Perhaps there was nothing burning near it, and it just didn't catch fire. Perhaps it was a miracle. I only know that the cross endured the tornado and the fire. Standing, holding the cross, I thought, "This cross endured, and I will endure as well."

A New Perspective

I have read stories of the amazement and wonder people experience when they regain their sight after being blind or partially blind. Experiencing a tragedy has brought me new eyes with which to see the world. It has brought a new perspective to many others, as well. In the South, churches are so common, they blend into the countryside. It is when they are gone that you realize that their presence somehow gave a sense of calm and security. We have found that when the church is threatened, even people who do not attend regard it with new appreciation. The church symbolizes stability in a community. Even though we may not agree with what some churches believe, we are glad that the church is present. The church has an air of divine presence.

What lay in the parking lot of Goshen United Methodist Church shook that sense of calm, and brought to the surface how much reverence churches inspire in our community. Lying in the parking lot was the church steeple. For years, it sat on the roof of the church, signifying that this building was built to glorify God. Even if those of us who attended church were not pointing to God, the architecture did so through this steeple with its cross. It was unsettling to see this symbol of power and majesty lying impotent on the pavement.

What was once high was brought low. The Christian story centers upon a God who willingly leaves a high place of glory and becomes a human being named Jesus. This human Jesus runs the risk of human fears and temptations. The irony of the high and mighty becoming lowly is baffling. By becoming human, God exalted humanity. "Where once we were no people, now we are God's people, a holy and royal priesthood" (1 Peter 2:9-10, author's paraphrase). The parking lot and land, once just a place to organize cars, was made a holy and sacred place as a broken steeple lay upon it.

People often ask me about my future plans. I laugh because I have trouble making long-term plans for my life and taking them very seriously. I no longer get as uptight over not reaching a goal as I did before. I try to experience the now.

I am intent on creating positive memories for children. I do not mind being silly with children. This Easter, I decorated a tree in our yard with large, colorful plastic eggs and large plastic bunnies. In previous years, I have made fun of these tacky decorations. Now, I see how happy they make Sarah, and say, "Why not?" As I was purchasing the decorations, the clerk at the store said, "Some people are beginning to decorate just like Christmas." I replied, "Well, why not?" In order to celebrate life now, it may take some colorful plastic decorations.

Before the tornado, I would think twice about riding on the slide with Hannah and Sarah at the park. Now I just climb the ladder and go down the super slide, not worried that I look like an overgrown kid. There are more important things to worry about than being caught having fun and acting silly with my children. Older people have often told me, "Enjoy them now, they won't be young long." I think about that statement more than most parents. I hope I never take my family or the symbols of the faith such as a steeple for granted again. However, I know how easy it is to slip into inattentiveness.

The Governor Visits

From inside the house, I heard helicopters landing. I was so tired I didn't go outside until I was told Governor Jim Folsom would like to speak to us. Kelly and I went to the carport and talked briefly with Congressman Glenn Browder. I had worked on Glenn's first congressional campaign, and call him a friend. Of course, friendships with politicians can get complicated. Glenn had come to the church on Palm Sunday after the tornado, looking for us, and had come back several times since. Kelly and he talked about the lack of a warning system in the area. In Jacksonville, where Glenn lives, and where we once lived, a siren system is in place in case of emergency. I was told that on Palm Sunday, it did not work.

Apparently the press had followed the governor; there were about twenty reporters and several camera crews there. One of the governor's aides is a former student of mine at Jacksonville State. We exchanged greetings, and he looked at me awkwardly. I told him that I was proud of him for getting a job.

Standing six feet, six inches tall, Governor Folsom is not hard to spot in a crowd. As Kelly and I went over to speak to him, the press closed in, making a tight circle. We shook hands, and our conversation showed that he was genuinely moved by the tragedy. I was looking up to the governor when I felt a camera poking me in the back. With the press closing in like a football huddle, our meeting felt undignified. There must be a better way for the governor to meet folks. He asked Kelly if there were anything he could do to help. Kelly urged him to acquire an emergency warning system. "If we had known there was a tornado, we would not have met. There was no siren out here," Kelly told him. "An emergency warning system of sirens could warn people in case of any emergency." The governor said that she had a good idea, and promised to look into it that day. Before the end of the day, most of the Alabama congressional delegation had joined the governor in sending a message to President Clinton and Vice President Gore seeking such an upgraded emergency warning system.

As we were leaving, a reporter asked me what I thought of Vice President Gore coming to visit us. I thought he was joking and said something about it being his job. I was certainly shocked when I got home that night to learn that Vice President Gore had asked to meet with us at the church the next morning. As soon as I heard he was actually coming, I regretted my comment. Unfortunately, a few news articles stated our ambivalence about Gore's visit.

At lunchtime, someone brought us some barbecue sandwiches. We sat in our driveway to eat. I brought Hannah and Sarah's wooden chairs from the carport. Hannah's chair had a ten-foot cotton rope tied to the bottom. The opposite end of the rope was tied to a stool. I explained to those around us that last Friday, before I left for Oklahoma, Hannah tried to make a tightrope and walk across it. Each time she would get the rope the desired four inches off the ground and would stand on it, the stool would turn over. I convinced her to walk on the rope along the ground. She tried it, but somehow the rope on the ground offered no excitement for Hannah. I felt guilty untying the rope from the stool, as if I was going against her will. In her honor, I left the rope tied to her chair. No one asked me why I didn't finish my task.

Some friends came by. Seeing them, I realized how badly I needed them and others in the Goshen community. We hugged and I cried. There it went again. It was strange how seeing a certain person causes my emotions to overwhelm me.

By three o'clock, we had loaded up my sister's van, my brother-in-law's van, and several truckloads of our belongings to take to the basement of the home where we were staying. The company had come with a U-Haul truck, and volunteers were busy loading our belongings for cleaning and storage.

The windows on one rear side of our minivan had been blown out, and I decided to take it to be fixed. I got in the van and started down the road. The van began to shake, and I wondered if other damage had been done to it. When I opened another window, however, the noisy shaking ceased. The vibrations had been caused by the pressure of air issuing through the broken rear window. I laughed at the simplicity of the problem. The next problem I saw would not be solved. In the van, there were two child's safety seats. A deep pain hit again as I saw Hannah's seat, knowing it would not be filled with her singing, happy (or sometimes cranky) self. I was alone, so no one knew I tasted salty tears.

Last Respects

That night we entered the funeral home with our family. Lying in the pink coffin, Hannah wore an aqua-green dress she had planned to wear on Easter. Her eyes were closed, revealing her long eyelashes. I touched her hand, her cheek. Death had taken away her softness. "Get up, get up!" I thought. Emotionally, I told Kelly, "I just want her to get up."

Kelly replied, "I know, I know." We hugged and shed some tears.

At opposite ends of the pink casket were a special doll and a favorite white stuffed cat. In the other parlor were photos, including one of Hannah and me at the beach. It expressed her joy at the ocean. Some artwork, including a paper angel and paint or crayon renderings of a house, flowers, a cat, some ghosts, and her family were displayed.

The funeral home staff was overwhelmed when over four hundred people came to show their respects to little Hannah. Many waited in line two to three hours to see Kelly and me standing beside the little pink coffin. Many told us later they wanted to do us a favor, so they left to lessen the load of our evening. After two hours, Kelly and I sat down for a little while. As I greeted people, I tried to say, "Be careful when you hug Kelly. She has a hurt shoulder."

A friend slipped an angel pin in my hand. Before we left that night, I pinned it on Hannah's dress. We also pinned a rainbow pin, and a pin depicting the universal sign language symbol for "I love you." We wanted to put her special golden cross, given to her by her grandmother last Christmas, in the coffin with her; but we couldn't find it amid the debris in our house.

I asked for some private time with Hannah before we left. I just wanted to talk to her one last time. One final time, I said, "Hannah, have I ever told you I loved you?" This time she did not answer, "Oh, Daddy, you tell me that all the time." But I knew that she knew.

Wednesday, March 30, 1994

The Vice President Visits

By six o'clock Wednesday morning we were heading back to Goshen to meet the Vice President of the United States. The mood in the car was excitement—it wasn't as if we were on our way to a funeral. This was a great diversion from it. When we discussed whether to go and meet him, Kelly said, "Why not?" It was a cold but pretty day as we awaited for the entourage including the governor, senators, congressmen, Agriculture Secretary Mike Espy, James Lee Whitt, director of the Federal Emergency Management Agency (FEMA), and probably others. The press were quietly waiting behind the tape, in their designated area, and the White House press office and security had everything planned. Along the road, rescue workers and some church members waited for the vice president to express his sympathy and his gratitude for their heroic rescue work.

The White House press officer briefed us on what we would do when the entourage arrived. I told him that I would like to make a statement to the press about the overwhelming support we were receiving. It was arranged, and the reporters were asked not to ask me questions. I walked over to where Vice President Gore would soon make his remarks and felt very lonely. As I looked out over the crowd of orderly, bored-looking reporters, I recognized many who had followed us all week. But today they looked disinterested. I did not know how to begin, so I stated my name and thanked them for allowing me to make a statement. "People have been so good to us," I began, "calling from all over the country saying, 'What can we do?' We're hurting so badly. But there are people hurting all over the country because of poverty, a lack of health care, and a lack of jobs. If you have been touched by this, I encourage you to find someone in your community and reach out and help them. There's so much love around. We just encourage people to keep loving better."

The White House press official told me it was a good statement, and I realized for the first time that when the vice president comes to town, no one would want to hear from a preacher. I felt pretty stupid and told him so as I laughed at myself. I was honored when a few papers ran parts of my statement urging people to reach out and love those who were suffering in their communities.

When Vice President Gore arrived, I was surprised at how many cars came in the entourage. Kelly and I walked over to greet him and walk with him over to meet our family and visit. I let him know that we had taken some flack for supporting him in the last election. He said he wasn't surprised about that in Alabama. We told him that we had gone to his inauguration, and this surprised him. He told us that we had shown great courage and been an inspiration to the whole country and commented that tragedies have a way of changing your perspectives on things. I shared with him that he had been an inspiration to me through the way he had handled his own son Albert's near-fatal accident when Albert was struck as he ran in front of a car. It was that accident that made Gore gain a new perspective about priorities. Gore stopped and looked at us for a moment. Then he emotionally said, "That changes things, doesn't it." Gore greeted all of our family and the district superintendent.

Kelly and I showed him the ruins. He had to help escort Kelly because she could barely see through her swollen black eyes. As we walked, Kelly described what had happened in the church. The governor, senators, and congressmen followed behind. For the press conference, we stood behind Gore, next to Governor Folsom. Gore's words were moving. Kelly silently cried when he said that her courage in counseling and helping others while dealing with her own grief was an inspiration to the nation. Gore said, "It is an experience of grace for our country that you have maintained your ability to lead your congregation."

According to newspaper reports, the decision to redesign the nation's emergency warning system was made during an impromptu government conference in the back seat of a limousine as Vice President Gore left the Goshen church. In the car with him were Agriculture Secretary Mike Espy and James Lee Whitt, director of the Federal Emergency Management Agency. The vice president used the car's mobile telephone to call the director of the National Oceanic and Atmospheric Administration in Washington, D.C. The four of them discussed what would be possible to warn communities at short notice. The vice president wanted to offer an immediate response to the forty-two deaths that resulted from the Palm Sunday storm. The next day, Gore announced the initiative to build one hundred new emergency radio broadcast centers, including a new tower for northeastern Alabama. The plan also calls for communications equipment that will allow emergency warnings to target specific areas. Gore said that this was a direct response to requests from Alabama for better warning systems. The towers would activate weather radios that households and people in public gathering places can purchase. Gore said he wanted these weather radios to become as common as smoke detectors. Joe Friday, the Director of the National Weather Service, came to the Goshen UMC on December 19, 1994, and dedicated the first of these towers in northeastern Alabama.

Self-Deception and the Hunger for Recognition

The attention and the kindness shown to us gave our pain a mysterious validation. Everyone treated us as though we were important people. I had a greater appreciation of how good that feels, especially when you are down.

I have to laugh when young children hide simply by closing or covering their eyes. They seem to believe that if they can't see you, you in turn can't see them. It is a minor flaw in reasoning, which they soon outgrow. I've watched turtles, frogs, lizards, and moths do the same thing. A frog sits on a lily pad, his dingy green color matching the color of the leaf. You can get quite close to the frog before it jumps. I imagine that it thinks it is hiding. The moth does the same thing as it lights on a tree trunk of similar color.

Just like the moth and frog, I too fell prey to deceiving myself. With all the attention of Holy Week 1994 I found myself thinking more highly of myself than I think was healthy. In talking about the interviews, I said to a friend, "Well, I wasn't the one talking here."

My friend responded, "That's right, it was God who was talking. It couldn't have been you."

At that moment I heard bells and alarms. It was a moment of self-realization. Of course it was God! How often are we tempted to gobble up praise like a hungry dog eats meat. In *New Seeds of Contemplation*, Thomas Merton reminds me that a humble man receives praise the way a clean window takes the light of the sun. The truer and more intense the light is, the less you see the glass. A humble person isn't concerned with himself or herself. Any good in that person comes from God. If praise comes, it belongs to God. Letting go of the illusions, the flawed self-conceptions, frees us from having to defend our reputation.

Hannah's Funeral

After Vice President Gore left, we told the policemen that we needed to hurry to make it to the funeral in Anniston on time. Several Piedmont police officers escorted our family quickly to Jacksonville. There, Jacksonville police picked up the caravan of cars and took us further. I could not believe that we made the usual forty-five-minute trip in twenty-five minutes.

Before the funeral, family members gathered in the chapel and prepared to go into the sanctuary. Many TV cameras and reporters were outside the church. We had determined that we did not want TV cameras in the service. We allowed one United Methodist media office to have a camera in the balcony. The sanctuary was full. Some estimated that six hundred people had come to say goodbye to Hannah, to show support for us, and to celebrate life, death, and the resurrection of the dead.

As we entered the large foyer of the church, we saw Hannah's art displayed on clotheslines. You couldn't get into the church without seeing those pretty watercolors and finger paintings. Kelly had chosen the art selections. She had also chosen a drawing for the front of the bulletin. Kelly remembered Hannah drawing it and saying that it was for her daddy. The typed title underneath the drawing made it look professional: "Fuzzy Bear with Balloon," by Hannah. The large bear had a belly button, a smiling face with ears and whiskers, and feet with claws. Along the side of the body were little short lines that made him "fuzzy." He was holding a balloon on a string. A flower was at his foot. I never imagined that Hannah's drawing would appear in newspapers and on T-shirts, and be distributed in church school classes for children to color as they talked about the preacher's little daughter named Hannah who died in the church. But it did. Some classes sent us the crayon-colored bears. Hannah would have loved seeing that. I hope she did.

We stood in the foyer while the music ensemble sang the selected songs. The first was a jazzy, a cappella rendition of "The Lord Is a Help, a Help in Trouble." Hearing this spirited music gave me goose bumps.

As the ensemble reached the climax in the chorus of the next song, "Give Thanks," the power and courage in their affirmation was evident:

> And now, let the weak say "I am strong,"
> Let the poor say "I am rich,
> Because of what the Lord has done for us." Give thanks, Give thanks.

The next song, "Think About His Love," emphasized that God's love can bring us through hard times:

> For as high as the heavens above, So great is the measure of our Father's love.

I thought this music would lighten the air and prepare us to truly celebrate Hannah's life. It did for me.

The pallbearers started escorting the little pink coffin down the long center aisle of the sanctuary. The congregation stood. The district superintendent, Herb Williamson, walked and spoke words from Scripture with authority:

> Dying, Christ destroyed our death.
> Rising, Christ restored our life.
> Christ will come again in glory . . .
> Jesus said: I am the resurrection and the life. Those who believe in me, even though they die, yet shall they live, and whoever lives and believes in me shall never die. I am Alpha and Omega, the beginning and the end, the first and the last. I died, and behold I am alive for evermore, and I hold the keys of hell and death. Because I live, you shall live also.

Kelly carried Sarah as we walked hand in hand behind the coffin. Kelly was wearing a black velvet dress and her blue shoulder brace. Sarah wore a borrowed multicolored jacket and clutched a bright yellow stuffed Big Bird given to her by her cousins.

The bishop shared with the congregation that we had just met with Vice President Gore, and he had given us a letter from President Clinton. He wanted to read it to the congregation. (Gore had thought the president had called us the night before. "We've been pretty busy," I told him.) The letter was simple:

The White House
Washington

March 29, 1994

Dear Pastor Clem:

I was deeply saddened to hear of the death of your daughter, caused by the devastating tornadoes and storms on Palm Sunday. Hillary and I extend our deepest sympathy to you and your family.

The destruction of Goshen United Methodist Church on this holy day is also tragic. We will keep you and the members of your community in our prayers during this difficult time.

Sincerely,
Bill Clinton

Bishop Fannin described Hannah's visit to his home in Birmingham. "When Hannah came to our house, she did not care if I was the bishop, but made herself at home, climbing and playing on the furniture and asking us if we had any toys. It did not matter to her that she was in the Episcopal residence. Hannah was just at home with people, full of life and energy. It was great, and we had a good time together."

Across the front of the sanctuary were more of Hannah's colorful, happy paintings and drawings. The largest was a four-by-two-foot white board on which she had painted a yellow sun, some blue clouds, and a brown circle for a person's face, including eyes and a smile. Legs and an arm with fingers extended from the face. Hannah was amazing. She had painted the board just a week before. Hannah and I were both helping my students paint an international mural in the Wesley Foundation lobby, and she wanted to paint her own painting. So I got her this white board, and she took the brushes and paint and painted a large masterpiece. She was proud of her painting, and so were the students. I enjoyed watching her grow up, and her art was part of that development. Circles were people. Eventually she was able to add two dots for eyes, a line for a mouth, then two lines down for legs. As she grew, she saw the potential for more details, such as two lines from the circle for arms and then little fingers off those arms. Hair consisted of squiggles, or just a few extra lines along the head. During her last eight months in preschool, she had learned a great deal. Her teacher told us how exciting it would be to watch her learn during this year, and it was. She practiced drawing houses and letters. It was a miracle to me to watch her learn.

A reporter asked Kelly if she wished she hadn't ever had Hannah, and Kelly responded emphatically, "*No*, I am thankful for the four wonderful years we have had together."

"Her Name Is Hannah" was the theme of Bobby Green's sermon. The sermon described the energetic, loving little girl who sang, danced, painted, and asked questions about God. You could tell that he knew her well. He described her as a happy child who graced and made sacred our lives wherever she went. He spoke of how Kelly announced Hannah's coming to the congregation at that very altar where Hannah's body now lay. Kelly had presented a music box toy that played "Rockabye, Baby," and in a children's sermon asked what it meant. One of the children guessed, "You're going to have a baby." Kelly said, "That's right."

He told of how he had guessed that we would name her Hannah with only Kelly's reference to an Old Testament woman who had trouble having children. Bobby said, "Hannah," and Kelly grinned. Her name was Hannah. He spoke of the time when Hannah got away during an informal worship service as Kelly was speaking and climbed upon the kneeling rail, embarrassing Kelly. Bobby said, "Kelly, that sacred altar was not blessed by the people who were married there or who prayed there, as much as it was blessed by Hannah's fingers and dance. It was Hannah's dance which made it sacred." Bobby spoke of Hannah's faith, how she described heaven as Disney World. Hannah understood that when you go to heaven, you live, and live, and live with God.

I was proud that Bobby's sermon had captured the exuberance of Hannah's life. I felt that all those gathered had the opportunity to know her and move from sadness to appreciation. It was a wonderful tribute. Later we would have a rainbow with the words "She Sang She Danced She Painted She Climbed" engraved on her grave marker.

We sang William H. Parker's hymn, "Tell Me the Stories of Jesus." Hannah loved the song and loved stories about Jesus and God. Hannah had sung this song and marched around waving her palm branches just four days earlier. On the third verse,

Into the city I'd follow the children's band,
waving a branch of the palm tree high in my hand . . .

I stopped singing as I thought of that verse being for her. I noticed that others stopped singing as well. It was a long time before I could sing much in church. I was beginning a time when others would sing for me.

The district superintendent led us in prayer:

God of us all, your love never ends,
When all else fails, you still are God.
We pray to you for one another in our need,
and for all, anywhere, who mourn with us this day.
To those who doubt, give light;
to those who are weak, strength;
to all who have sinned, mercy;
to all who sorrow, your peace.
Keep true in us
the love with which we hold one another.
In all our ways we trust you.
And to you,
with your church on earth and in heaven
we offer honor and glory, now and for ever,
Amen.

We sang Natalie Sleeth's powerful hymn of death and resurrection, "Hymn of Promise." During this hymn, Kelly and I both thought of the pansies Hannah had planted just a few weeks before. We thought of how much Hannah loved butterflies. And we clutched to the hope that was carrying us forward, that indeed, through this winter season, a spring would come:

In the bulb there is a flower; in the seed, an apple tree;
in cocoons, a hidden promise; butterflies will soon be free!
In the cold and snow of winter there's a spring that waits to be,
unrevealed until its season, something God alone can see.

There's a song in every silence, seeking word and melody;
there's a dawn in every darkness, bringing hope to you and me.
From the past will come the future; what it holds, a mystery,
unrevealed until its season, something God alone can see.
In our end is our beginning; in our time, infinity;
in our doubt there is believing; in our life, eternity.
In our death, a resurrection; at the last, a victory,

unrevealed until its season, something God alone can see.

I still can't sing this song without thinking about Hannah's pansies. Although we were not living at the house, they kept blooming and blooming all summer long. It was as if Hannah's spirit was giving us a sign of her ongoing life and the blossoming of her new life.

Sarah sat still for a while, looking around the sanctuary. We showed her the paintings and drawings that Hannah had done. She was interested for a while, and then grew restless, but her grandmother had some diversions that kept her happy.

We left as we had entered, following the pink coffin with pink roses on top. The congregation was singing William W. How's great hymn, "For All the Saints":

> For all the saints, who from their labors rest
> who thee by faith before the world confessed,
> thy name, O Jesus, be forever blest.
> Alleluia, Alleluia!
>
> O blest communion, fellowship divine!
> We feebly struggle, they in glory shine;
> yet all are one in thee, for all are thine.
> Alleluia, Alleluia!

As we were leaving, Sarah walked between Kelly and me, holding both our hands. I couldn't help grinning with pride and joy for the lovely service and all the friends who had come to the service. The congregation sang as we walked down the aisle. It was as it should be, for when death takes away your song, the community can sing and pray for you in your grief, filling the silence. It was just the beginning of how the church would reach out and care for us. In looking out at the crowd, I regretted that our departed friends at

Goshen could not attend; and I wished I could have attended their funerals.

As we were driving through Huntsville, I started to become very nervous. Kelly and I sat in the back seat, while Kelly's sister, Natalie, sat in front and her husband, David, drove. I looked over at Kelly. She didn't seem to be feeling the emotional pain I was feeling. I thought, "I guess shock is a great protector in times like this. Let me have some more!" By the time we turned into the cemetery, I had begun to panic. "I can't do it—I can't say goodbye," I cried to myself. It was the same panic I'd felt on Sunday night upon arriving to see Kelly and upon first seeing Hannah lying in the coffin in her aqua-green dress.

The car door was opened. A hand extended—I hesitated. Then I noticed that I was getting out and walking. Someone wrapped a warm coat over my shoulders. A freezing rain began to pour. Kelly was at my side, and a woman from the funeral home was leading us to our place under the tent at the graveside. "Nature Herself Seems to Grieve for Young Victim," ran a headline in the next day's Huntsville paper.

About two hundred mourners gathered in the cold, wet, windy cemetery. I felt sorry for our friends who had traveled all the way to Huntsville, and for those who were standing out in this cold, wet weather. They were all sorry for us. "I guess we're just a sorry lot," I thought to myself. My uncle came from the hospital to be with us. I noticed police officers on the road and later learned that they had stopped film crews from entering the cemetery. The police had also given the hearse carrying Hannah's body a police escort to the cemetery. Hannah would have loved the attention and flashing blue lights. She knew police officers were her friends, but also that they would reprimand her if she were not buckled up in her car seat or seat belt.

A white teddy bear was at the center of one of the sprays of flowers near the small pink coffin. Herb Williamson said,

"Hannah showed us life and the presence of joy. She taught us how to live victorious every day." Then he prayed:

> O God, all that you have given us is yours.
> As first you gave Hannah to us,
> so now we give Hannah back to you.
> Receive Hannah into the arms of your mercy.
> Raise Hannah up with all your people.
> Receive us also, and raise us into a new life.
> Help us so to love and serve you in this world
> that we may enter into your joy in the world to come.
>
> Into your hands, O merciful Savior,
> we commend your servant Hannah.
> Acknowledge, we humbly beseech you,
> a sheep of your own flock,
> a lamb of your own flock,
> a sinner of your own redeeming,
> Receive Hannah into the arms of your mercy,
> into the blessed rest of everlasting peace,
> and into the glorious company of the saints of light.

Bishop Fannin said, "Hannah lived a life of wide open arms, and she was always there to embrace you. Now I can see the arms of the Creator embracing her. She loved life and touched us all." As we were leaving, I threw some dirt and flowers into the grave. I could not say goodbye.

Many of these same hymns, Scripture lessons, and prayers were sung and spoken at funerals all week.

Thursday, March 31, 1994

The next morning, we assembled family members at Hannah's grave. The sun was out, and it was a pretty day. We picked out some flowers to press in our Bibles. I walked over to my parents' graves and silently said, "Now you watch over little Hannah. I can't do it anymore."

Kelly gathered everyone around the grave and said, "I have something I want to say. I want to thank you for loving Hannah because love is what it's all about. You loved Hannah, and she was happy. Loving is what it's all about." That was all.

Kelly and I agreed to meet for lunch at the Wesley Foundation after she visited the hospital and attended a triple funeral. The Foundation was adorned with flowers that people had sent us. We decided that one gift we could give to the church members in the hospital was an arrangement made from the flowers people had given us. Kelly's Aunt Laura and her mother were good at making arrangements, and they made around thirty flower arrangements that afternoon. Our Wesley Foundation students divided the hospitals up by city, and different groups delivered the flowers to eight different hospitals. These students were nonstop workers.

Saturday, April 2, 1994

A stained-glass artist from Largo, Texas, had called. He had finished four stained-glass windows for a Roman Catholic church and wanted to donate them for our Easter sunrise service. After he had spoken with my secretary several times, I spoke with him personally and gave him the go-ahead to send the crate air express. His description of the four pieces did not prepare me for the beauty of these four wonderful works of art. How we would display the stained glass was a problem. We would have to build a frame and install it before Sunday. I began looking for a carpenter to build a frame with a cross in the middle. We could hang the four stained-glass windows in each of the four sections created by the cross. We could cover the side beams with chicken wire and on Easter morning fill it with fresh flowers. I drew my plan out on a piece of yellow paper. No one around us seemed to have a better idea.

I don't think that it was by chance that Kelly's old friends from northern Virginia showed up to help. I found out that he could build things, and he readily agreed to build this frame. On Saturday he bought the wood, screws, and wire for the frame. He worked all morning installing it. Some international students showed up and were happy to go to the hardware store to get some chicken wire and do the scratchy job of cutting and putting it up. I was pleased at their willingness to work on this Christian symbol, for one was Hindu. The Hindu student graciously attended the Easter sunrise service.

On Saturday, hundreds of volunteers were clearing the downed trees and burning debris. We had to clear the area for the Easter sunrise service. I kept asking people where they were from. Many were Baptists from around Alabama. Some were members of the Holiness denomination, and others were Methodists.

"Who coordinated this cleanup effort?" I asked.

"Nobody. We just knew there was work to be done, found a place, and started," they responded.

What a wonderful way to help, I thought. Just go to the need and start helping. I appreciated their initiative.

Our front yard was cleaned off by the time I got there. Volunteers were trying to fill in the craters left by the downed trees and smooth the ruts made by different trucks and cars.

The twisted jungle in our backyard was also being cleared of debris. A tremendous hole left by a fallen tree was hard to fill. I noticed a rope and swing still tied to a limb lying in the yard. I went out and told a woman, who seemed to be working with her husband, that I would like to have that swing and rope. A few minutes later she found me, and as she handed me the swing and rope, I knew she knew that Hannah had enjoyed swinging on this swing. Hannah had often shrieked with joy on this swing. I had made it and hung it myself to create a long, high tree swing. Many times I had stood on the edge of the sandbox, and as she had swung toward me with her mouth and eyes wide open, I had pretended to try to reach for her before she swung back. She would swing away from me, anticipating the return threat, and scream with joy. Now, the four-by-fours used to hold the sand in the sand box were broken and scattered around the yard. The sand spilled over into the dirt.

As the workers raked and cleaned, they used the little red wheelbarrow that had remained undamaged through the storm. I had to grin as I watched them use it. They had no way of knowing what a symbol of faith it was becoming for me.

Easter Sunday, April 3, 1994

No one spoke in the darkness as we gathered to prepare for the service. Momentarily, car headlights shone toward the wooden frame and cross, giving some light by which to work. The darkened stained glass hung with phenomenal beauty. Family members arrived and silently began to weave things into the chicken wire—flowers from the graves of their loved ones; a small United States flag. All I remember was the heaviness of the moment. I remember thinking about the women who came to the tomb that first Easter morning with spices to finish embalming Jesus' dead body. I imagined that they walked in sad silence, yet they had a responsibility to fulfill in order to honor the dead. Many people were coming, but in the darkness, speaking would have been somehow sacrilegious.

The congregation sat in folding chairs in the parking lot, facing the rubble of fallen red bricks, damaged red pew cushions, and the downed black roof resting just a few feet off the ground. The rustic wooden cross stood in the rubble of the old sanctuary. Broken concrete blocks supported it. It was this rustic wooden cross that was to be used for the crucifixion and resurrection in last week's drama. The stained glass and newly constructed cross and flowered frame stood as a translucent backdrop on the edge of the rubble next to an orange plastic "keep out" fence. Our house was at the rear of the congregation. A huge, nine-foot oil painting of Jesus walking on the water was hung on the side of our house and framed the setting for the Easter sunrise service. An artist from Mississippi had just finished the painting and thought we needed it, so she had delivered it herself.

About two hundred people gathered for the service. They came in wheelchairs and on crutches. Bandaged, bruised, and with red and black eyes, the people of Goshen came, eager and hungry to hear the Easter message of hope and resurrection. With them came the hopes and dreams of the thousands of people who had been touched by the tragedy they had witnessed through the media coverage. All those prayers, thoughts, and feelings descended upon that sacred piece of broken land. During the week, Kelly had told me, "It is really strange, but while we were in the midst of digging people out of the rubble, and trying to keep one another calm, we were living the Holy Week story. We knew that Easter and hope were the end of the story, and in a way, knowing, even subconsciously, that this was not the end of the story kept us going." The sun rose above the eastern mountain range as the congregation began singing "Because He Lives." Like most things in this setting, the song took on new meaning.

> because I know he holds the future,
> and life is worth the living just because he lives.

Our two-year-old Sarah wouldn't look. She kept her eyes closed and stayed in her grandmother's arms throughout the service. At first we thought she was asleep, but she wasn't. She would not look. It was her first time back to the church site. She had not talked for several days. She had built towers with blocks, and with a wipe of her hand would knock the tower down saying, "Church fall down." She would not look at the fallen church on Easter, but she heard the strong voice of her mother say, "I wouldn't be anywhere else today. Would you?" Then Kelly read with courage and power from Romans 8. Two nights before, Kelly was not sure what she would do in the service other than talk with the children.

Kelly awoke one morning with the words from Romans going through her mind, and she knew that she *must* read these words during the sunrise service. She felt God had spoken to her with this message.

I consider that the sufferings of this present time are not worth comparing with the glory about to be revealed to us. For the creation waits with eager longing for the revealing of the children of God. . . .

. . . If God is for us, who is against us? He who did not withhold his own Son, but gave him up for all of us, will he not with him also give us everything else? . . . It is Christ Jesus, who died, yes, who was raised, who is at the right hand of God, who indeed intercedes for us. Who will separate us from the love of Christ? Will hardship, or distress, or persecution, or famine, or nakedness, or peril, or sword? . . . No, in all these things we are more than conquerors through him who loved us. For I am convinced that neither death, nor life, nor angels, nor rulers, nor things present, nor things to come, nor powers, nor height, nor depth, nor anything else in all creation, will be able to separate us from the love of God in Christ Jesus our Lord. (Romans 8:18-19, 31*b*-32, 34-35, 37-39)

A soloist with a strong baritone voice sang:

We are standing on holy ground,
and I know that there are angels all around.

The music sent shivers across my arms and chest. The soloist was one of my Wesley students and had helped clean up the debris and had found the organist's three-ring binder of music wet and filled with concrete grit. The organist was touched when he brought it to her cleaned up and restored. This was indeed holy ground, and surely, those new angels—Hannah, Amy, Jessica, Jonathan, Zachary, Eric, Diane, Earl, Buddy, Derek, Kay, Ethelene, George, Kirk, Freddie,

Cicero, Ruth, David, Michael, and Cathy—were looking down from heaven on us gathered in this holy place.

The thirty-minute service brought together the community, most of whom had not seen one another since the tragedy. We had all been busy at hospitals, funerals, and cleaning up during the past week. People kept saying, "I'm praying for you. It's all I can do." The support that came from others and God really gave us courage and power.

There were many hugs and tears as congregation members greeted one another. Members of the First Presbyterian Church in Piedmont provided a generator for electricity to work the sound system and helped with chairs. The Cumberland Presbyterian Church, located just down the highway, hosted a breakfast following the service, where a congregational meeting was held. The bishop and district superintendent, as well as the Red Cross representative, spoke briefly during that meeting.

Before Kelly and I went to the breakfast, we had agreed to do an ABC live interview behind the church. It was very cold, and as we waited, I was shivering. One of the men in the camera crew took off his heavy coat and insisted on wrapping it around my shoulders. I was touched at his care and amazed at the coat's warmth.

The sound man said, "Here we go," and counted down with his fingers as another man took off our overcoats so that I could appear in a suit and Kelly in a dress. Those interviewing us set the stage and asked about the service and Kelly's injuries. The interviewer then said, "Another question that many people are asking is Why would a benevolent God allow something like what happened last Sunday to occur? What do you tell your parishioners when they ask you that question, especially on Easter week and on Easter Sunday, when so much is about rebirth and joy in the Christian church?"

I responded, "It is also about death and passion, you know. We believe very strongly in a loving God, a loving

God that has a natural world which has tornadoes and tragedies all the time, and we do not think God has anything to do with that. And that's what we believe. It was a tornado that destroyed this church. And it is a miracle that 125 people were not killed when you look at the destruction and rubble. So there are many heroic stories of people taking care of one another, and I hope some time we will be able to share some of those stories with others; because so many people gave their lives, literally, for other people, and there were many miracles.

"We lost our four-year-old, and we are going to miss her so much, and that is painful. And it brings Holy Week to life for us. We have talked about suffering for years during Holy Week and cried with God losing a child. And we have really experienced that this week, and so we understand that a bit more. But the good news is that the resurrection is here. And we celebrate Easter, even though we feel like we're still in the tomb, and we may pray with Jesus, 'Let this cup pass from us'; but we know that Easter is coming, and that is good news. . . . You don't need faith for the things you understand. You need it for the things you don't.

"Ten years ago, I couldn't have talked about the theology of suffering. But in the last ten years, I've experienced the death of both my parents, a fire to the home in which I grew up, a miscarriage, and the illness and death of a brother-in-law. Especially the death of my father in 1983, when I was only twenty-four, caused me to deal with grief and why bad things happen to good people. Grief was not a stranger to me. What I spoke in the interviews about God suffering with us, it was not some sentimental hopeful faith, but a faith that was forged in the trial of pain and suffering. When I said that we would survive and that Easter would come, I spoke out of my experience that grief and pain do pass and we move on as new creations."

That evening, we were gathered in our temporary home. Sarah rode on the huge stuffed yellow duck someone had given her. Three different Easter baskets surrounded her, and she spread the little green and purple shredded plastic grass and plastic eggs on the den floor. People had been very kind to give her stuffed animals and toys for Easter.

We heard a knock at the front door. I opened it, and to my surprise, there stood my old friend Arlene. She had learned of the tragedy while in Guatemala, when she had seen a crowd of mothers leaning over and reading a newspaper in disbelief. She wanted to know what was causing such an emotional response and crowded in to see the story of the tragedy of children and people being killed in a church in Alabama. She was saddened. She kept looking at the article, and grabbed the paper from the women's hands when she realized who the story was about. Then her feelings changed from sorrow to pain. Her plane had landed in Birmingham just a few hours before, and she came straight to us with a letter.

The letter contained her memories of the tough little two-year-old Hannah who had explored Yellowstone National Park with Arlene and us. At one point Hannah was running to the car after seeing a geyser, and she fell, scraping her face and hands. She cried a little, but then she was ready to run and explore some more. I loved these personal memories Arlene shared with us in writing.

There were boxes of mail yet to open, and about ten packages had arrived. I was feeling loved and experienced a spirit of gratitude. I decided to open the package that was wrapped most attractively. I felt like a kid at Christmas. I opened the box, and inside were more nicely wrapped gifts. I opened the one on top, a framed verse of encouraging scripture. I thought, "That's nice." The scrawling writing on the attached note said, "The best is yet to come, keep looking." The next wrapped gift was a framed happy rainbow with the words, "Joy in the Lord." Another attached note said, "THIS IS A SPECIAL MESSAGE FOR REV. CLEM, YOU MUST LET HER SEE THE MESSAGE AT THE END." This was getting a little strange. Underneath this gift was a printed booklet full of Bible verses. The attached message here was threatening, "YOU WILL ROAST IN HELL IF YOU DO NOT GIVE REV. CLEM THE MESSAGE BELOW." This message startled me, but I opened the last gift in the bottom of the package, and in big red letters was the message, "REV. CLEM, YOU ARE LEADING PEOPLE TO HELL. GOD DESTROYED SODOM AND GOD DESTROYED GOSHEN. GOD DOES NOT LIKE WOMEN PRETENDING TO PREACH THE HOLY WORD OF GOD." Down below this was another warning: "If you keep this message from Rev. Clem YOU WILL BURN IN HELL."

Attached to this handwritten note were about five pages of typed scripture passages that described God threatening retribution for wickedness. Highlighted in yellow were passages of Paul's words in the New Testament that forbid women to speak in church.

I felt dirty and sick. I packed all the gifts back into the box and took it to the trash can. I felt I needed to wash my hands, hoping to cleanse myself of this sick person who went to all the trouble to send this misleading message of love and damnation. I knew Kelly's family had opened up letters they called "sick," but they had thrown them away rather than giving them to us. I did not tell Kelly, but I described to her dad what I had opened. He just shook his head and said, "There's a lot of sick people in the world." I did not risk opening any other mail that night unless I recognized the name and address on the envelope. I couldn't take any more rejection.

Today I saw a pine cone fall to the ground. It bounced, rolled, and settled on one spot. I'm sure pine cones fall often, but have you ever witnessed it?

Only once before do I remember witnessing the fall of a pine cone. I was younger and sitting outside with many friends when a falling pine cone plopped in a friend's lap. As he jumped, we all laughed. The timing was just right. Today, I drove around the curve at just the moment it fell. My eyes were open, and I noticed it. I saw the pine cone just before it hit the ground and then jumped.

I thought it was a pine cone, and then I doubted. Maybe it was a jumping frog. Then I said, "No, I must trust what I saw—it was a pine cone."

Many important things in life depend on timing.

Falling in love might come several times, but making a commitment to get married depends upon timing.

Does the timing of when we are born make a big difference in our lives? Certain seasons and circumstances make big differences.

Seeds are planted, and the ground is refreshed by good rain, and new life sprouts.

Seeds are planted, and the hot sun bakes the earth, and potential life is stopped. The pain comes at one moment. The doctor is in, or the doctor is out, or there simply isn't a doctor. Available medical care that can treat the pain makes the difference. The timing of the illness makes a difference.

*In a classroom or more than likely in a hallway outside, a particular word is spoken **and** heard. It is the word that will help a student make a decision. This particular word is life-changing.*

A song is sung, and a dream is renewed or a commitment remembered.

From the pulpit, a word slips out. It surprises the preacher. The preacher regains control and speaks from the prepared text. The word that slipped out was an answer to someone's prayer.

Highways are dangerous every day, and we practice highway safety each day. In spite of our preparedness . . .

    the slick tires
    the patch of ice
    the look that did not see
    the dangerous driver . . .
It all depends upon timing.

We can practice safety if we are aware of danger ahead of time; but often the timing and predictions aren't precise enough, and we are caught off guard.

An earthquake causes a bridge to fall and a building to cave in. A tornado smashes a church full of worshipers, and a flood quickly rises to your ceiling.

Small decisions mean life or death. Where you sit or stand—whether your apartment is on the first or the third flood. Whether you stand or kneel, whether you turn to the left or right, whether you drive your car through the water or wait for the water to subside.

Many of the most important decisions we make in life have much to do with timing.

I knew what a friend was going to say before he said it. As soon as he said, "It's all in—" I could finish the phrase. He had said it so many times it made me start flinching when the sound "all" rolled off his lips: "It's all in God's plan."

I believe that God can do whatever God desires. And God desired not to make everyone's decisions—big or small—for them. God does not choose for me to eat an ice cream float at bedtime, or tell smart missiles which house to destroy or when to misfire. God does not determine the timing of every raindrop's fall or the intensity of storms. But God is aware of all these things, even the falling of a sparrow or the number of hairs on our heads.

Jesus said that God knew when each sparrow fell, but did not say whether the sparrow fell because it was hit by a rifle's bullet, or because it was caught in a tornado, or because its nest washed down a swollen river.

I do believe God and the spiritual world can help us prepare for the storms and for the timings of life. God listens and cheers us as we make decisions that move us to wholeness and growth.

God's timing means that God doesn't worry as we do about the meaning and reasons for things that are affected by timing.

Ultimately, God's timing is bringing creation into wholeness. God started creation, and as the creation nears completion, God will complete it. God's timing is bigger than we can imagine. This *does not diminish the love God has for each of us, or the significance of God's act of love in becoming a human himself in Jesus, and experiencing life, death, and life.*

What is lasting according to Paul is faith, hope, and love.

Does the falling of the pine cone fit into God's timing? Does a flood, earthquake, car accident, or death because of tornadoes fit into God's timing?

God cares very deeply about what happens, and through whispers and nudging and perhaps even through the dropping of pine cones, God can bring us healing, growth, and wholeness through our guilt, pain, and grief.

The Week
After Easter

Children and Death

I stopped by Hannah's preschool on Monday morning to discover that the teachers were helping the children deal with their friend Hannah's death. As you would expect, the teachers and her friends were pretty shaken. They had read a story about death and then they each had shared what they remembered best about Hannah and made colorful drawings. The teachers wrote on the top of each drawing a description of what that child had drawn and colored, then fastened the drawings together in a booklet and presented them to me. I had greeted many of these children for almost two years, and they knew me as "Hannah's daddy." The director told me that the children would love to see me. So I visited several classes, received hugs, and talked to the children. The director said that personally seeing us would be an important part of the children's healing.

Sometimes I still take out Hannah's class picture. Some faces are smiling, some bored, some distracted. It is a typical group of four-year-olds. I look at the picture, locate the individual children, find the picture they colored, and think about what they remembered. One came to the funeral home before the crowds to give Hannah a picture of himself so she would always remember him. His mom nervously told us, and we thought it was a great idea. He had drawn a slide and colored the entire page green and written, " . . . we play together and have fun."

Another said, "I will always remember Hannah because we play parade together." He drew three colorful people with their arms extended, wearing hats. Four of the children drew monkey bars with smiling colorful figures and backgrounds. One said, "I will always remember Hannah because she waits her turn on the monkey bars." I wondered if it were true. Many of these children colored Hannah's clothes pink, her favorite color.

One colored a tire swing and another drew a swing set. Still another drew Hannah wearing pink with green angel wings and said, "I will always remember Hannah because she swings with me." Other children remembered skipping, coloring, and sliding with Hannah. The booklet is a real treasure for our family.

Over the next few months we learned about how children deal with grief. Our friend Hanna Schock drove from Birmingham each week to work with the children in Goshen as a part of a support group. She and the First United Methodist Church of Birmingham had created suitcases full of activities and toys to use in helping children deal with displacement and disaster. There were colorful children's books with stories of children who cried when their parents were killed or who lost their house in a fire. Sarah's favorite was one where a mother was crying over the loss of a child. Sarah would look at the picture over and over and say, "Mommy crying. Mommy crying. My mommy cries." Each week she would go to the suitcase and find this particular book and the particular page and stare at the picture of the crying mother.

In the suitcase was a blanket designed with a simple, colorful town complete with roads, a hospital, a fire department, a church, a school, and houses. There were toy fire engines, an ambulance, and other cars. Children could use the toys and act out the tragedy through play. I suspect they needed to tell the story just as we did, but lacked the words.

So they played it out over and over again. The children would use blocks to build the church and then knock it down. Then the fire trucks came along with the ambulance. A doctor's kit helped the children act out what they remembered and experienced with the injuries.

The counselors used puppets to help the children act out scenarios of the tragedy they had experienced. A chart with sad, happy, angry, confused, and crying faces was designed for children to identify their feelings. Crayons, paper, scissors, glitter, glue, and stickers gave the small group of children a way to express what had happened through art.

We found it critical to take the grief of the children seriously. Their grief was real. Several adults shared with us that when they were children, a sibling had died and their parents hadn't wanted them to be sad or grieve. They had to wait until they were adults to realize they had unresolved grief to deal with. At Hannah's preschool, the children built a small flower garden on the spot where Hannah loved to play. A sign reads, "Hannah's Corner." They have a small chair there so children can sit there and think. Hannah's playmate Hannah Morgan was very sad after her death and would tell her teachers she just needed to rest and think for a while. She would sit in the chair next to "Hannah's Corner." It was a wonderful way for adults to help provide a space and invitation for the children to deal with grief.

The children were very concerned about another tragedy occurring again. In our support group we discussed how to respond when our children asked us if another tornado could hit our church or house. How do you respond? Would you say, "I hope not"? That may not relieve the fear of the child. Do you respond with honesty and say, "A tornado could once again hit the house, but we are watching the weather, and we will be safe." When Sarah asked, I began saying, "Sarah, we are not going to let anything happen to you." I love William Stafford's poem "With Kit, Age 7, at the Beach,"

in which his seven-year-old daughter questions the heart of
the father:

> We would climb the highest dune,
> from there to gaze and come down:
> the ocean was performing;
> we contributed our climb.
>
> Waves leapfrogged and came
> straight out of the storm.
> What should our gaze mean?
> Kit waited for me to decide.
>
> Standing on such a hill,
> what would you tell your child?
> That was an absolute vista.
> Those waves raced far, and cold.
>
> "How far could you swim, Daddy,
> in such a storm?"
> "As far as was needed," I said,
> and as I talked, I swam.

Celebrating Children's Spirituality

It is no small thing to be chosen and marked by a child. It
happens in many ways, but two days before the tornado I
watched it happen as Hannah and her class visited with
elderly men and women in the Jacksonville Recreation Center. Hats decorated with colorful silk flowers and ribbons
adorned the heads of the fidgety children as they sang "Here
Comes Peter Cottontail." The children were encouraged to
speak and give stickers to the seniors at the center. The man
Hannah chose sat very still, looking straight ahead, barely
aware of the noisy, active children's presence. His vacant
eyes glanced downward as Hannah's cheerful voice an-

nounced, "Here's your sticker. Happy Easter!" Hannah carefully placed the sticker on the back of his hand. He never moved or spoke. When she finished, Hannah looked at Kelly and me for approval. After receiving no response from the man, Hannah moved on to another task. She gave stickers to Sarah, Kelly, and myself. I expected her to comment on the man she had just marked, but she took it all in stride, as if the best way to give a gift is not to expect an affirmation of your gift.

I am sure that like that old man, I have been marked by Hannah in ways I will never know. She has given gifts I've never acknowledged or even realized she gave.

Not long ago, Sarah was sitting in my lap during a worship service. Sarah had received some stickers in the children's sermon and had placed one on the back of my hand. I remembered the sticker as I walked forward to serve Eucharist. I started to take the sticker off my hand, and then resisted. "It is no small thing to be chosen and marked by a child. It is perhaps the greatest gift one can have," I thought, as I held the chalice of grape juice and said the words: "The blood of Christ poured out for you." I remembered the day when Hannah had placed that sticker on the hand of the old man. He did not do anything to deserve Hannah's sticker—it was simply a gift. "The blood of Christ poured out for you. It is a gift," I overheard myself saying.

What is it about our children that helps them to be our greatest teachers in life? One of the first steps in realizing that our children can be teachers is simply treating them with respect and as persons whom God through the Holy Spirit and through experiences of faith is shaping. Hannah asked me once, "Is God a person?"

"Yes, but God is more than a person, God is a Spirit."

"Like the wind and sun?" Hannah asked.

"Sure," I responded. "God is near to us like the wind, and warms us like the sun. The sun comes up every day to remind you that God loves you. So when you see the sun, remember that God loves you."

"Oh," Hannah answered, as she ran off to give her baby a bottle.

The rain ruined Sarah's plans to play outside, and she asked her mother, "Did you make it rain?"

Kelly answered, "God made the rain."

"Oh," Sarah said with a sad face.

I thought Sarah would be angry at God for ruining her day of play. I could not help but add "God made the earth where all kinds of weather comes, the rain and the warm sunny days, as well as the snow. But I don't think God said, let's let it rain today."

Sarah did not listen to my further explanation. I guess I was defending God for myself. Did Sarah really accept the idea that God made it rain? Did she think that God wanted it to rain today and ruin her day of play outside? I don't know what Sarah thought, and I did not think to ask her. But I am sure that if she is like the rest of us humans, she feels that she has a unique relationship with the world.

Is it true that God made it rain? The answer is yes and no. Yes, God created this fragile earth with seasons and weather. Did God specifically choose a particular cloud to unload on a specific piece of earth or people? I don't think so. But then again, it could happen.

God is like the wind, but not like the whirlwind that killed Hannah. God is like the nice warm sun, but not like the intense heat in the desert that scorches and kills. With all the disclaimers, are we capable of constructing a language and creating experiences that draw us deeper into an understanding of God, or are we so limited in our understanding and vocabulary that we know only that God is for us and not against us?

Hannah was a spiritual seeker. Two things were very clear about her search for meaning and God. First, she worked hard to gain an understanding of God and how and why life worked. Second, she approached this spiritual quest seriously and enthusiastically. Her trust and sense of wonder about her life were both refreshing and threatening.

Hannah talked to God regularly and imagined what God was like. I believe that as she reached out to eternity, eternity reached in and touched her. I was amazed by her excitement about God and church. I know I underestimated the spirituality of children before the tornado. I was fascinated with Robert Coles's research on the subject in *The Spiritual Life of Children*:

> "I was all alone, and those [segregationist] people were screaming, and suddenly I saw God smiling, and I smiled," one North Carolina girl of eight told me in 1962. Then she continued, with these astonishing words: "A woman was standing there [near the school door], and she shouted at me, 'Hey, you little nigger, what you smiling at?' I looked right at her face, and I said, 'At God.' Then she looked up at the sky, and then she looked at me, and she didn't call me any more names."

I think we can take the spiritual experiences of children seriously. Perhaps children are more in tune with the possibilities of the supernatural than those of us who are ruled by reason and cause and effect. For one thing, children are connected to whatever they do more than we are. When Hannah drew a picture, she usually drew herself in the picture. She approached God and everything with the enthusiasm of connecting herself with the reality.

If we went to a beautiful mountain, Hannah and Sarah would enthusiastically shout about how big it was and how beautiful it was. They would wonder if it had caves, bears, and tigers. I would probably think about "conquering" it by climbing it, or perhaps even owning a piece of it. When it comes to God, I am trained to try to figure out God, conquer or please God; whereas Hannah and Sarah would be happy to enjoy God. If a friend was healed from an illness, Hannah would simply say, "I'm glad you're feeling better"; and I would try to figure out a reasonable explanation.

If God can communicate God's love and support to adults, why not children? The peace that passes understanding does just that. As much as Jesus said about children, I suspect that they may have more experiences with eternity than we can imagine.

Sometimes I have idealized the wonder and amazement of a child's faith. Hannah valued wonder over information. I have wished that I could have the innocent faith that believes without asking so many questions. However, when I think of all the questions Hannah asked over and over again, showing me that she was not satisfied with the answers she received, I wonder if children have more complexity to their thoughts than the innocence I idealistically project upon them.

It is easy to see children like Hannah as simply children rather than as real people who are truly seeking God. My adult knowledge leads me to think that years of experience hold all the wisdom concerning the ways of religion. However, I realize I don't have all the answers, when a child like Hannah or Sarah asks, "Why are there snakes?" The pat answer, "Because God made them," would not satisfy Hannah's curiosity. I can still hear her intense question, "But why?" Perhaps a more thoughtful response would be an answer that fits snakes into the purpose of creation. "If there were no snakes, we might forget to watch where we step as we walk through the woods. Without snakes we might forget to notice the beautiful flowers, snails, and all the wonderful things that are on the ground. If the fear of snakes did not cause us to be cautious on our walks through the woods, then we might be in such a hurry that we would fall in a hole, or trip and fall. Snakes cause us to slow down and live a richer life."

In response to the question, "Why is the sky blue?" instead of saying, "Because God made it that way," I could answer, "Let's look at it again. Are you sure it's blue? Let's look at the sky at sunrise and at sunset. Let's look at the sky tomorrow, and the next day. Let's look at the sky during a storm. The sky has many moods just as you have many moods. The sky is not only blue but pink, red, orange, white, black, and gray. Looking at the sky is like going to a different artistic perform-ance every day. God made the sky for us to enjoy. The wind cools us in the summer and blows seeds for trees and flowers for new flowers. The winds are sometimes dangerous as they are blowing things around. The winds blow the clouds that are filled with water from place to place, watering the earth, filling the streams and lakes, and watering the plants." If I were to go into such a long explanation to Hannah, she would have probably gone back to climbing before I finished the story. But at bedtime, she would be a captive audience. Perhaps these explanations would put her to sleep.

Reporters kept the question of "Why?" in front of Kelly and me. "Why did your daughter die? Why a church?" Sometimes, I would answer them with another question, "Why were we born in the first place? If we can figure out the mystery of why we are here, then we might have some clues to the mystery of why we die." The question of the meaning of life is a search that haunts the young and old alike.

I can understand why we would dismiss the spirituality of children as simply fantasies and ways to understand difficult parts of life. There is cruelty in the world, so we have witches, bad guys, and evil empires. I have thought to my-self, "Hannah believes that Mickey Mouse is a real character who is alive. She believes Santa is real. How can I claim that she has a real spiritual life when she is so easily charmed by what we tell her or don't tell her?" Perhaps there is power in the ability to believe and reach toward eternity. The images of Mickey Mouse and Santa are certainly real, just as the images of those we elevate as heroes are real. But the images that are projected about heroes and saints are only part of their identity. The images' limitations don't make them meaningless.

Children have the ability to bring out the child in us and remind us to play. Playing is important in our search for wholeness, and it is a wonderful gift to receive. Hannah taught me to play.

Can play be a way to reach toward eternity? Just two weeks after the tornado I had an alarming dream that Hannah's funeral was a high-tech production. The funeral took place in a gothic cathedral, like the chapel at Duke University. There were huge video screens placed down both sides of the cathedral. There were lots of sound and video wires running along the side aisles. The cathedral was full of people. The funeral began and there were film clips from Hannah's life, accompanied by music performed by famous musicians. I did not think that it had any cohesion. The sequence and music and film made no sense. A lady behind me loved it, and told me that it made perfect sense to her. She leaned forward to explain, "You think you live for goals—but God works in play." I awoke, wondering how God worked in play.

The painful and refreshing theme in the New Testament says that we must become as children if we are to enter the kingdom of God. Were these apostles saying that we adults become so "wise" in our maturity that we forget to ask questions and refuse to be seekers? Was Jesus saying that the way a child approaches life and the world is something that we adults have lost? Has our education taken away our ability to approach life and the world with respect, awe, and wonder? The comment raises many questions: What is it that children know that I don't know? How can they trust in ways that I cannot trust? How do they approach the world differently than I approach the world?

I don't think that Jesus was saying that children are cute and vulnerable, but that they are God's messengers and sensitive to spiritual things we can only imagine.

The Beach

Signing up at the Red Cross for help was difficult. Admitting that I was in need went against the grain of how I was raised. The first question asked of us was, "How many in your family?" Kelly couldn't answer. It was the first time Kelly had to say, "Three." Tears filled her eyes as she just stood there looking off into space. Somewhere on the forms she had to list that Hannah had died in the tornado.

We left the Red Cross and drove to Gulf Shores, Alabama, for a week to rest. We loaded our white minivan with boxes of mail and a few clothes and took off for recreation. The week was spent not only resting and opening mail, but trying to make sense of what had happened to us the previous week.

One of my favorite times to walk on the beach is at sunrise. The sounds of the crashing ocean and the quickly changing colors are quite dramatic. One morning I watched the sand quickly change from hues of pink to orange, and finally to white as the dawning sun rose. The white foam of the surf reflected hues of pink and orange, as well as shadows of green and blue. The constant crashing and receding of the waves gave comforting rhythm that somehow seemed to become synchronized to the rhythm of my breathing.

Busy sand crabs ran sideways across the sand. High tide had washed up a shell with a tentative hermit crab peering over the opening. The glory of the sights, smells, and sounds caused my spirit to soar, then the realization of joy was interrupted by a twinge of guilt. Feeling joy seemed disrespectful to the dead. I thought, "Maybe Hannah will send me a message today." I looked around for a dolphin, a bird, a shell. There is always hope that something will speak to me of her new life. I saw sand crabs scurrying, sea gulls flying low, and six pelicans hovering and diving. "Where is a message from Hannah, or God?" I am drawn back to the hermit crab tentatively poking his eyes around the edge of a small shell.

Like me, the hermit crab grows and must look for a new home. Is he well practiced in hanging on as the rough waters shove and push his tiny shell? Now stranded, washed up on the shore, is he home or does he wish to be back in the water's current? He appeared vulnerable and frightened out of the water. He watched me look at him. I stepped forward, and he retreated into the shell.

Like a homeless hermit crab, I too felt as if I were washed up on the shore, my home, my life wrecked by windy currents. I asked, "Who am I now that my world has changed?" I wondered if my eyes looked as frightened as that little crab's. "What shell can I retreat to for protection? Who am I now that I have no shell, and now that everyone is looking and watching, with eyes of pity. What do I do with myself? Once, a great deal of who I was was wrapped up in teaching Hannah, playing with Hannah, having hopes and dreams for Hannah. Who am I without Hannah always asking me questions? I am still a father, but without that child. How can I be a full father without Hannah? I had such hopes for Hannah's future. I wanted to teach her to make a difference in the lives of others. What do I do with this emptiness, this void? Thank goodness I still have Sarah and Kelly." The rhythmic crashing of the sea awakened me to this prayer:

> Take me, O God, and rock me in your ocean. Surround me in your bosom and hold me tight.
> Rock me with your eternal rhythm of the waves,
> for I am like a child, in need of your healing
> and care. Amen.

In my journal, I recorded:

like a hermit crab
looking for a new shell—
the last one broken, shattered

A shell is security
    meaning
    a way to see God and the world
    home.
I'm looking for a new shell
    Can I patch up the old one
        or must I begin anew?
'tis glue and grace which holds the shell together.

The notation of that day ended, "We eat a meal, and where is the one to lead the prayer? Where is the one to be climbing as dangerously and high as she could? What will I do now without her? Sarah now has a big responsibility—to lead the prayers at mealtime, to get the attention, to initiate play and songs without big sister's constant motion. I miss those sacred moments so much. I love you, Hannah. Nothing to do but cry."

Where Are the Tears?

A pine cone was in a bowl in the middle of the table in the house at Gulf Shores. The pine cone's little branches were fully extended. Just a few weeks earlier, Hannah had worked very hard to rescue that pine cone from about one foot of water. She used a crabbing net, lying on her stomach on the dock, reaching over the side of the dock and trying to capture that pine cone. She was very proud of it and shrieked with joy when she finally held it up in the net. She insisted on taking the pine cone into the house. Its tiny branches were tightly closed around the center. I explained to her that as it dried, the pine cone's branches would reach out. Upon seeing the pine cone in the bowl, I remembered Hannah's joy at capturing it and her anticipation of seeing it change forms. It had changed over the weeks. She would have liked that. I thought of my own life, and how Hannah had come into my life and helped me to reach out just as she had transformed that pine cone. By fishing it out of the water, she helped it to become what it was intended to be. She had helped me to become what God intended for me as well—she had taught me to love. I closed my eyes and tried to remember everything about Hannah's life. I wanted to never forget all the memories. I kept thinking, "These memories are all I have now."

In my journal, I began to list things I remembered about her life. The hospital delivery room where she was born and my pride at cutting the umbilical cord flashed before my closed eyes. After Hannah's birth, Kelly shrieked for joy. I had no words, but I stood there beside them both and applauded. When Hannah was only hours old, I began to rock her, and I asked the nurse if rocking her was safe. She laughed and warned me that I'd better be careful because the baby might get used to it. I smiled as I remembered how unprepared I felt to care for a baby. I remembered bringing her home from the hospital, and insisting that the crib sit beside the bed. I watched this two-day-old baby during the night, afraid that she might stop breathing. I remembered the time when as an infant she was sick, and I spent the night holding and watching her labored breathing, afraid something might happen. I thought of how much trouble and energy Kelly put into nursing and reading about the stages of development. I remembered the hours I spent rocking her and singing her to sleep. Memories of her life up until the last goodbye flashed in my mind like a fast-paced movie. I cherished them all like I had never cherished anything before. My love for those small times with Hannah made their remembrance more painful.

I wanted healing tears to fall. But during the week we spent at Gulf Shores, my tears dried up just like my feelings, hopes, and happiness. Where there had been feelings of occasional strength and inspiration to get through the week before, I now experienced only extreme exhaustion. We moved slowly and painfully, but the wailing did not come— it was as if our bodies were tired of crying and moved into a time of existing as if we were barely alive.

The Parachute

Kelly and I took walks together on the beach. On one of our walks, we saw a large crowd of about forty people gathered outside a condo with cameras pointing up toward the sky. The group was excitedly pointing up and covering their eyes to look toward the sun. Kelly and I were curious. Surely this many people would not be pointing to an imaginary sight high in the sky merely to attract attention, as my friends used to do in high school. Kelly and I strained to see something in the air but saw nothing. I thought that it was perhaps someone parasailing, but I couldn't find a boat or a person parasailing. Kelly and I kept walking closer. We looked up for an airplane, but all we saw were puffy, white clouds. Finally we saw a tiny figure. We watched this tiny purple figure become a purple rectangular parachute, carrying two people riding piggyback. We just stopped and watched them glide around and around. We nervously looked around to see where they would land. The beach was quite windy, and not many sunbathers dared to lie out. One lady was stretched on her stomach on her lounge chair. She was not far from the noisy crowd, but she never moved. It was as if she was sleeping in the midst of the chaos of the crowd and the spectacular sight of the graceful parachutists. The cameras were rolling, and the crowd was cheering as these two people got closer to land. I wondered if they would have enough control to land properly in such a strong wind from the sea. I felt my body tighten with anxiety as the parachutists neared the ground. They were heading right for the sunbathing lady who had never looked up to see the commotion. I was amazed that someone so close to an event that forty folks and now many others had gathered to watch could be completely oblivious to what was going on around her. The parachutists landed smoothly about twenty feet from the sunbather. The purple chute collapsed within ten feet of the bathing beauty—but she never moved. I was relieved that they had landed safely and had missed the unaware spectator. The crowd rushed forward. The two flyers were unstrapped. Congratulatory hugs and hand-shakes followed. The cameras continued to roll as the purple parachute was folded into a backpack. The sunbather never moved. I imagined the comic video commentaries that could show the elegant flight of the parachutists and the undis-turbed repose of the sunbather. "Here they come, and will she notice? No, not yet. You can hear the crowd begin to cheer louder as they get lower." (The camera shows the parachut-ists, then comes back to the sunbather.) "Will she move with the increased noise from the crowd? Apparently not."

In some ways during the previous week I had felt as if Kelly, Sarah, and I had been pushed out of a plane and were falling into a pit of despair. But somehow the grace of God had become our parachute and upheld us. I wondered when we would land. When we got into a new home and felt settled? When we moved to a new place? After one year?

I remembered the many hugs and pats on the back, and people telling me, "It's okay, everything is going to be fine." Were they trying to offer hope or avoid the pain? Everyone wants a quick fix and to be back to normal. I knew that the grief I had after my parents died lasted for years, and I knew

Hannah's death felt much worse. I knew that working through your grief isn't quick or easy. It is a slow journey; patting a grieving person on the back and saying, "It's okay," is similar to telling the parachutists as they jump through the plane door that their landing looks good.

What about the woman so close to the parachutists who missed the whole thing? In some ways, since I missed the tornado, I was like the sunbather, who was close to the event, but missed it. Perhaps there is a message in the tornado that is obvious to everyone else, but I am missing it. I kept praying, "God, Hannah's death is too devastating and painful for me to miss any learning or message. Please help me to make some sense from this absurd situation!"

My fellow clergyman W. G. Henry always said as he introduced a speaker, "All your life, you have been preparing for this moment." I knew without a doubt that God had not caused the tornado to hit the Goshen church, but I began to wonder if indeed all my life I had been preparing to deal with tragedy and suffering. I had buried both my parents, a friend, a brother-in-law, and seen my childhood home damaged by a fire. I had seen hopeless poverty in the United States and in other countries. The weekend before Palm Sunday I had spoken on a religious retreat for young adults, and shared about planting pansies with Hannah and Sarah, as well as about learning from my children. I had also said, "If you forget that God loves you, the sun will shine in the morning to remind you. And if in the nighttime you are suffering, then the moon will come out and remind you of God's love." I spoke of the book of Job, and how we must learn to rely on God and not other things such as material possessions—how we must learn "to rest in God." These words haunted me. They echoed in an empty cavern.

I thought of our dealing with the press, and felt shame because I enjoyed feeling important. "They've got my number," I thought. "Treat me like I am important and special and I'm hooked." I hated that my insecure ego needed

WINDS OF FURY, CIRCLES OF GRACE

approval every few minutes. It felt good to be treated like we were important, but in the back of my mind, I knew that this could be a weakness rather than a strength. The confident side of my personality responded to the comment "All your life, you have been preparing for this moment," by thinking that indeed I had learned a language to discuss suffering because I have dealt with it a lot. The less confident side of my personality kept following two avenues of questioning: "How do I look? How am I doing?" and "What will I do to try to be important? Will trying to feed my ego lead to my undoing?"

Kelly and I tried to bring meaning to the whirlwind we had experienced in one week's time. Our homelessness was a nagging irritation to me. I felt that it was my responsibility to provide a home for my family. When the week was up, I was ready to get settled. If I had known how many months, how much energy, and how many people it would take to arrive at a "settled" state, I would have been overwhelmed. It seemed simple—find a house, move in, get some furniture, fill out insurance forms, and rearrange our belongings that were now being stored and cleaned. What a foolish assumption!

The Mail

While at Gulf Shores, we sorted the mail into stacks after each letter was read. Three small envelope boxes were used to sort checks with the appropriate designation: Church, Clem, and Hannah's Playground. We thought we would get caught up on the mail with a week at Gulf Shores, but with four adults constantly opening mail, we did not.

We received several books on grief from authors, friends, and strangers. Joan Haines, an author of children's books, sent Sarah five of her "Rosie Posie" books, complete with

"Rosie Posie" stickers. Most of Sarah's toys and books had been taken away for cleaning, and she enjoyed her grandfather singing and reading from these Rosie Posie books. It was a timely gift. Many of the letters began, "I've been crying for two days." There were many letters from clergywomen across the country. Kelly said, "I think every clergywoman in the United Methodist Church has written."

As we opened letters, we made stacks separating the letters we appreciated from strangers, and those from friends, and the "sicko" letters. Fortunately the letters of comfort and encouragement greatly outnumbered the "sicko" letters twenty- or thirty-to-one. Sometimes the letters in the "sicko" pile were addressed to the leaders of the Goshen congregation. Kelly's parents tried to screen the letters and save Kelly and me the pain of opening them. It would take about six or eight positive letters to clear our minds of the haunting evil in the tone of the negative letters. However, over time, we grew tough skins and didn't take these letters so personally.

Hundreds of letters and phone calls came from people who provided services and wanted to help in the rebuilding process. It was hard to know if those calling wanted to donate their services or sell their services. Because there were so many, we eventually gave a member of the church the responsibility of handling those offers. In the early stages after the tornado, we received many offers of pews, carpet, storm shelters, organs, wood, roofing shingles, heating and cooling systems, but most turned out to be salespeople trying to sell the church their products. Rarely did someone make a written offer that we could deal with; most made their offers over the phone. After we returned their long-distance calls, we realized that they wanted to sell us insurance, grave markers, lightning rods, storm windows, as well as other things the new church would need. Some, however, did want to give their services and donate merchandise. I don't want to be too quick to question whether these people's intentions were honorable or not. I prefer to think that they were truly moved by the tragedy and saw that they had products they believed could help. Wanting to help was what motivated many people to call and send information on how the church could raise money by selling products such as candles, candy, pumpkins, and Christmas trees. Selling these items could be rewarding, and even provide us with the "blessings" described by the salespeople, but they were low on our priority list when compared with the tasks that concerned us such as burying the dead, finding a bed to sleep in, encouraging people in the hospital, and keeping a scattered and broken congregation together.

I wish I were a poet and could express how helpful and supportive the mail we received was. It was like a huge security net that helped hold us up and let us know that we were not alone. We could not help but be touched by the tender letters in which strangers shared their own painful journeys of losing a child through death. They knew our grief and gave words of encouragement.

The Wind

We thought Sarah would enjoy getting back to the beach, a favorite playing place. However, when we first took her to the surf, the wind was rough, and the noise of the ocean frightened her, and she cried and had to be held tightly. She would not open her eyes for fear. We immediately realized that the wind and noise must have triggered memories of the tornado.

Flashbacks due to wind, storm, and noise were common for the survivors. Panic was common each time there was a loud noise or a storm. During the night a thunderstorm moved through with thunder, lightning, and strong winds. Kelly panicked and suggested that we go and sleep in the hall.

I preferred to look out and watch and listen to the storm. Kelly asked, "Do you think you would have time to run and get in the hallway with us?" I nodded yes. With tears in her eyes she said, "You just don't understand. There was no time for us to move before it hit. The tornado was moving so fast that we had no time to run." I will never understand or have the flashbacks that those who were in the midst of the tornado do.

Sarah's fear was typical among all the children and adults who had survived the tornado. Many shared that their fear of the unlikely was greatly heightened. Imagine yourself standing beside a tree and thinking, "This tree could fall on me." Imagine yourself in a crowded wedding reception, looking outside to see rain beating against the window. You look back at the crowd and imagine individual persons struggling to pull themselves from the fallen building, with bloody faces, arms, and bodies. You wonder what they would look like lying dead in the front yard. Next, you make your plans for reaching the safest space, and wander over close to the inner closet or bathroom. We would enter a restaurant or public building, and if there were no outside windows, we would not stay long. Survivors and even I still have a great fear of not being able to see outside. In most places, Kelly and I both figure out the safest place to be in case of a tornado. Sometimes we joke with each other after we leave a place and say, "Quick, where was the safest place you planned to dash in case of a tornado?" We usually have planned the same places, and only occasionally have we realized that neither of us made a plan. Over time, this preoccupation has subsided.

The Myth of Safety

The morning sun had climbed quickly to the southern sky. The ocean was glassy and calm. The gentle breeze from the

Gulf made it a perfect day at the beach. As I ventured out into the waves the water was more refreshing than shocking. I stood motionless, feeling the rocking of the ocean on my legs, and gazed along the endless horizon. I thought about the whales and different creatures that lived in the ocean. I turned and headed back to the shore and felt stings along my thighs. Jellyfish. I had walked into jellyfish. Even on the calmest and prettiest of days at the beach we run the risk of jellyfish, seaweed, or biting flies, sunburn, or powerful waves.

"It shouldn't be that way" I moan. "Why must there be such annoyances?" The truth of the matter is that if you walk into jellyfish, they will sting you. If you pick up a copperhead or rattlesnake by the tail, it might bite you. If you grab hold of a rose bush, it will prick you. All these things hurt us because it is in their nature to hurt. The earth is like that. It can't help but hurt us. Life is like that too; by living and loving we can't help but be hurt.

We walk into a building, and with wide eyes Sarah turns to us and asks, "This building gonna' fall down?"

We answer, "No, we are safe."

She is not convinced and asks, "Is a tornado coming back to get us?"

I answer, "No, we are watching the weather." We feel safe because we now have weather radios and are supersensitive to the weather. Yet earlier this month, tornadoes went through Arab and Joppa, areas not far from us, and due to technical problems such as lightning, the warning was not given. A four-year-old girl was killed, while sleeping in the security of her own bed.

With all our warning systems, we create a false illusion that we can protect ourselves from suffering, pain, and death.

Fairy tales often end "and they lived happily ever after." Jesus said, "You shall have tribulation." But then he went on to say, "Be of good cheer, I have overcome the world" (John

16:33 NKJV). In other words, coping is possible. We would like to believe the fairy tale rather than Jesus' words.

We in the Goshen community are constantly aware of the possibility of danger. As we see planes flying overhead, we think to ourselves, "That plane could crash on my car or into my house." It could happen! The impossible has happened before! When we have these thoughts we feel silly, but our naive trust has eroded away. One family's house in our community was destroyed in a tornado that hit on February 27, 1993. It took all year to recover and rebuild. They had just moved in when the March 27, 1994, tornado destroyed their new house. It could happen! It could happen again!

In our community we have been working to get a siren warning system in case of bad weather. Many families have built storm shelters and stay in them religiously during bad weather. One family's storm shelter constantly fills with water during storms. They have joked, "Now we have to decide whether we want to drown or get blown away." Taking precautions is necessary and to neglect such precautions would be foolish.

Some people, such as Ernest Becker, claim that our culture's obsession with safety could be considered a denial of death. In his book *The Denial of Death*, Becker describes that one way we deny death is through "self love," or compulsively doing everything we can to busily make our lives more important, make a difference, be heroes, manipulate and control others. Another way of denying death is simply becoming paralyzed and projecting our need for protection to something outside ourselves—God, a psychologist, a pastor, a siren warning system, Strategic Defense Initiative, the NOAA weather radio, high-tech health care, intensive care beds in the hospital.

According to Will Willimon, with all our huge investment in death denial through high technology, "Americans die younger, lose more babies, and are at least as apt to suffer from chronic disease as those living in other industrial nations that spend much less on medical care." In *The Search for Meaning*, Willimon asks, "Have we ever encountered a high tech weapon system we did not want to buy?" We spent eleven trillion dollars on the cold war.

One Goshen tornado survivor said that he gets his family into the basement during bad weather. In Vietnam he learned that if someone was shooting at you, you got down. To do otherwise would be foolish. I am not advocating that we live foolishly and jump into tanks full of sharks, handle rattlesnakes, or refrain from visiting the doctor when we are sick. What I am advocating is that denying and avoiding the reality of suffering and death does not teach us to live fully. Facing the reality that the world is dangerous and that we cannot always protect our children from harm is facing the honest and painful truth. Facing this truth sets us free to live more fully in the present.

Before I realize I have walked toward the glass door, my hand is turning the knob. I am not sleepwalking, but I am moving and listening as if in a dream. Each step is slow and deliberate, allowing my bare feet to become anchored on the wet, glistening deck, now exposed by morning light. It isn't the hazy beams of first light that has brought me to the deck; it is the singing.

Her whole body sings as she lifts her head upward and moves from limb to limb. Her stunning black feathers shine, accenting two distinct red markings behind her head. It is not my presence that makes the bird nervously shift within the bush, for I cannot tell if she ever notices that I am near. Perhaps the bird is possessed by the passion of the song and doesn't even realize her movements. Never have I heard such a loud voice from such a small creature. Never have I been brought so close to a bird so captured in such a passionate song.

My transfixed eyes are not six feet away from the source of joy that fills the deck and echoes through the valley. "Who is this bird?" I wonder to myself. The constant movement and passionate speech seems familiar. Has the spirit world brought this tiny creature to this deck for some greater purpose? I notice that my heart is beating more quickly than normal. My spiritual heart is filled with the joy of this small messenger.

"What wisdom are you bringing me?" I think, hoping the bird could hear my question. The bird is singing, and my ears hear, but the sounds are meant for the heart and for levels of existence yet unknown. I can see many other birds gathering seeds and singing the joys of morning, but they are together as a flock, and they watch me as I draw closer. Where is this bird's partner? To whom does she sing with such gusto? Are some birds called to sing alone, while others are satisfied within the flock, singing quiet songs muffled by the bush where they hide? Is this bird searching for meaning?

The questions are endless. Debra keeps asking me, "Why didn't I die in the tornado with my boyfriend?" My answer makes perfectly good sense to me; she was sitting where the wall did not fall, and was protected by the roof. Those who died were simply in the way of flying blocks, roofs, beams, and tons of cement. She happened to be out of the way. She doesn't hear my reasoning, but keeps asking, "But why didn't I die?" Would it help if I yelled, "Because you were flat on the ground under a bench that did not collapse, and you had room to breathe!" No, it wouldn't satisfy this question, because she is asking a more eternal question: "Why am I here?"

It is the same question I ask of the singing bird who nervously shifts only a few feet from my hands. So possessed by her question, Debra ignores my reasoning. What is the song or message that possesses the bird to ignore my presence?

The cool morning air causes my body to shudder, and wakes me to ask myself the question, "Why am I here? God, where are you calling me? Why was I born? What am I to do?"

Was this bird given a song to sing from within her spirit or from beyond herself? Was it learned or did it come as a gift?

Each of us is looking for a song, a voice, and a place to sing. Why was I not killed with my loved one? My song is silent—it was snuffed out by rocks and wind and rubble.

"Little bird, are you singing for me when my voice is silent? Did you bring me outside this morning to remind me of joy, color, and beauty? Is this why you are here?"

Perhaps this purpose alone would be enough; but certainly there is more reason for our lives than to sing, to add color and beauty. Is it not the connection I feel with creation that makes my heart burn? Is it not the peace I feel as I watch my children sleep? Is it not the pride I feel as I watch and listen to my wife gracefully speak and love?

The wood is cold and soaked with the night's wetness. My chilled feet turn to leave the bird to sing alone. Debra must find her own voice, and so must I. The bird has found its passion, and so must we. My heart follows my feet in turning. It is not easy turning away from brokenness. The concrete, glass, and wood have been burned and buried. Will I let my passion and song be burned and buried with it? My feet are turning and walking away, and my heart is following.

The sun is rising, the sky is pink, and I am leaving tracks in the wet grass between rows and rows of blooming flowers. I turn back and see my footprints. The tracks are very prominent now, but within an hour, they will simply disappear. Small spider webs clinging to the earth sparkle and shine like jewels along the ground. I am tempted to grab the jewels, or with one sweep of my foot wipe out a spider's home. I keep walking.

I hum the first verse of the hymn "All Things Bright and Beautiful" before I realize I am humming. It is as if my heart is singing to my mind and body. I smile and let the rhythm dictate my step. I walk down a hill, and up another. And then, I repeat the process as I arrive at yet another new place. I pause in my walking to notice more spider webs glowing in the sun, and more blooming flowers. Only on my return walk do I notice that I have not walked alone. A bird has followed me. Is it the same bird whose song lured me out to the deck and prompted me to ask questions? The sun has quickly moved up into the sky. As I near the house, I stop and look at the bird and ask again, "Who are you, little bird?" I know stories about ravens bringing food to Elijah. I saw a wonderful stained-glass window at a monastery once that told another story of ravens bringing food to a monk. The bird's beak points to the sky and gives out a loud call, and she flies away without looking back. It is as if she isn't even aware of my question or stare. I turn to leave with the questions still in my mind. "Was God visiting me in that bird? Was Hannah visiting me through the bird?" Drawn into the mystery of life, I retreat into the house, refreshed for another day.

Angels, Heaven, and Mystery

Greeting us on the refrigerator at the house in Gulf Shores was a butterfly Hannah had drawn and colored just a few weeks earlier on a previous visit. When we saw the butterfly, knowing that it symbolized resurrection and life after death, I couldn't help but stop and think, "Is this a sign? Did Hannah's subconscious know something I didn't know?" It fit in with Hannah's preoccupation with death, tornadoes, and heaven in the weeks prior to her death. Hannah was very much interested in talking about what happens when we die. While she and Hannah were planting pansies, ten days before the tornado, Kelly explained that some flowers come back year after year after they die, and some flowers, like pansies, had to be planted each year. Hannah thought about it and asked, "Will Mr. Marcus come back then?" Marcus, a retired leader in the church, had died the year before. Hannah missed "Mr. Marcus." Kelly explained that when you die your body dies and goes in the ground at the cemetery and your heart goes to be with God. Hannah wanted to know what heaven was like, and Kelly said, "It's like the best thing you can imagine." Hannah thought for a while, and it was then that she asked if heaven could be like Disney World. Kelly said, "Sure." Hannah did not let the conversation about death and heaven drop, but brought it up several more times. The Friday before Palm Sunday, as I drove her from her preschool in Jacksonville to Piedmont, Hannah talked intensely about tornadoes. She knew what to do in case of a tornado, but did not understand how they could knock a tree or house over. The wind was blowing our little red Volkswagen Fox, and I pointed out the strength of this wind. I told her a tornado could blow our car over. She said, "But how?" I tried to explain that the winds are so fast and strong they can blow over trees and houses. I reminded her of the broken trees she had seen after a small tornado had come through our community a year earlier. She remembered the woods with cut off trees. "Remember the smell of broken trees at our house?" She nodded as if she remembered.

Why would a four-year-old be so intent on talking about death, heaven, and tornadoes?

Earlier that day, both Kelly and I had decided to attend Hannah's preschool Easter parade with Sarah. We both felt that we needed to be there and support Hannah as she and others wore their flowered Easter hats, parading and singing Easter songs around Jacksonville's town square. We had never both attended the school's parades together before. Kelly took Sarah, and Hannah was so proud of her little sister. She took Sarah by the hand and led her from store to store. Sarah was touched by Hannah's life, too. Hannah told all the friends in her class that Sarah was her sister. When Sarah grows older, she will treasure the videotape we made that day of her big four-year-old sister, leading and caring for her at an Easter parade, wrapping her arm securely around her as they sat on the floor and sang, only two days prior to her death.

I began asking crazy questions: "Did Hannah know on some unconscious level that she was about to die in a tornado? Did some part of Kelly and me know we needed to spend more time with her and make ourselves take time and attend the Easter parade?" I wondered if I were making these connections out of my grief, or if there were other signs that the disaster was coming. I thought I went to Hannah's Easter parade because I knew I was leaving for a week, and wanted to show Hannah I supported her before I left town.

Why had I been haunted by thoughts of a coming disaster? I had attributed it to paranoia after losing both my parents when they were only fifty, and my brother-in-law when he was thirty-five. I remembered the words I had said to myself on Saturday night after the powwow in Oklahoma, "When I have my disaster, I will shave my beard as a symbol of grief." I realized that for months a growing fear of a looming disaster had been part of my psyche. As soon as I had this thought, I thought I was imagining something. This was on the edge of weirdness.

A friend later reminded me of a conversation we had had months ago. I had told him about dreaming of an owl in May of 1993. Being part Cherokee, I felt the owl held a meaning from my Indian heritage. I asked a Native American minister about my dream. Fear filled his eyes, and he began to back away. Then he asked me what kind of owl it was, and I described the owl. He did not want to tell me the meaning, but finally said, "The owl, in many Indian traditions, is a symbol of death. The owl comes in and steals the baby's soul. There are many legends that say when you dream of an owl, death will visit your family." That night in May of 1993, I called home to check on my family. I was glad to hear Kelly's happy voice. They were fine, and I wondered about the meaning of the dream. The scare did not go away. Had I had a strange feeling for a while that death was coming into my life? My friend reminded me that I had shared with him an irrational fear that something bad was going to happen to my family.

Surely, I thought, my grief is just inventing these strange occurrences and memories. But the door in my mind was open to the possibility that the mysterious world of God, angels, and the communion of saints could give us hints of upcoming events. I am a person who believes that prayer does not just affect the psyche of the person praying, but actually makes a difference in the "next world," which makes differences in "this world." I firmly believe that God is whispering and speaking to us all the time, and we learn how to listen and see the signs and voices of God. With this understanding and appreciation of the power and presence of God, it only makes sense that God and God's angels can give us guidance and counsel.

Hannah was certainly a spiritual child who loved God, who prayed and believed God heard her prayers. Jesus and God were her friends. Could God have helped her and us to prepare for her death by causing her to ask questions and urging us to attend the Easter parade?

John Wesley said that Methodists "die well," and it was certainly true of many of those who died at Goshen. One member of the congregation told me that her husband had begun to act differently in the last year before his death. He started to prepare and take care of things in their house he had neglected for ten years. He had called a brother with whom he had had a strained relationship and reconciled. The week before his death, he was possessed with an urge to finish deeding his son some land. A woman who died had told a relative in her last few weeks that she was ready to die at any time. One young man and his girlfriend had become serious in their relationship in the two weeks prior to Palm Sunday. It was as if he had decided that it was time to declare his love and express his hopes for the couple.

Were these changes in people's lives and conversations taking on unexpected meanings as a part of our attempts to make sense and bring order out of the unexplainable? Were these actions out of the ordinary at all? Or was it simply that in light of the disaster, details and conversations of the preceding few months took on new meaning?

Kelly and I spent hours talking about these strange occurrences and their meanings. In my mind, I was able to conclude that, indeed, God may choose not to interfere with the straight paths of a storm, but God can prepare us for what will come. God can help prepare those who died, perhaps not with explicit, conscious awareness that death is near, but with some subconscious level of awareness. Such preparation could have helped make the death a smoother transition. Yet this reasoning doesn't explain all accidents and deaths. Any reasoning can lead us only so far into the mysteries of God's plan and life.

Hannah's Gift of a Rainbow

One of the last days we were in Gulf Shores, we went to eat at a restaurant overlooking Perdido Bay. It is a lovely place, where the Bay connects with the Gulf. A fabulous tall bridge goes across the bay within a hundred yards of the state line, connecting Alabama with Florida. As we were finishing our meal, a hush went across the restaurant. We saw children running to the windows with amazed faces. The once noisy restaurant quieted as if everyone were taking a moment of reverence. We heard that a double rainbow had appeared before we saw it. Kelly ran outside and I joined her. Kelly began to cry. Her tears were tears of amazement and overwhelming joy. She gave me a hug to the side without taking her eyes off the rainbow. "This is Hannah's rainbow," she said as she sniffled and batted her eyes to see through her tears. She held Sarah on her side and we watched the amazing double rainbow. Kelly felt Hannah's presence as she saw the rainbow, and knew without a doubt that Hannah and nature were sending a sign of peaceful presence.

Hannah loved rainbows. Kelly and I explained to Sarah that Hannah was in heaven (the sky) and had made this rainbow for us. Within a week, Kelly, Sarah, and I were driving and saw another rainbow. Again, an overwhelming presence and happiness filled our hearts with joy. Hannah was sending another rainbow for us. Sarah enjoyed the sign that Hannah had sent us. After that, she began looking for rainbows herself.

On many occasions, Kelly and I have experienced awareness of Hannah's presence. We have both questioned whether it was coming from our imagination or from a different level of existence.

I began to think about life after death. It was a subject to which I had given a casual nod all my life. In college I was irritated by the uninvolved attitude persons in the church held about trying to improve the conditions of the poor. They sang of how good it would be after death, and I worked like a crusader to improve conditions for people now—in this life. I remember thinking and saying that life after death was not important, but what was important was how we lived today. Remembering this statement sent a pain of shame through my body. Suddenly, life after death was more important to me than many things. I had to know that Hannah was alive and that someone was taking care of her.

Our Christian faith speaks of life after death. Even unbelievers admit intuition; the volumes of research on near-death experiences, as well as stories and mythologies throughout history, point to the reality that what we now know as life is not all there is. Are there spiritual realms and spirit worlds we do not understand? The Christian faith, which claims that death in this world moves us to a different form of existence, is a comfort to me.

Connected to the Universe

Because of the rainbows and other experiences of sensing God's presence, I began to think about how we are connected to nature and God. Faith connects us with God, other people, and the universe. God is able to touch us through ourselves, others, and nature.

Two consecutive mornings, I awoke to two birds outside the window at my bedside singing loudly on the windowsill. I immediately woke up and thought, "Hannah is waking me up." She used to wake me up often with her singsong chant, "Daaad-dy, it's wake-up time." Why did I sense her presence? Was I projecting this from my unconscious need to see her? Perhaps, but nonetheless, I sensed her presence in the form of the singing birds. This leads me to the question, "Can Hannah through the spiritual world influence birds to sing on my windowsill and wake me up?" It sounds crazy, but the answer is "of course"; we are all connected. The connections draw us into the greater mystery.

Our connection to God and the universe allows me to let parachutists, hermit crabs, and rainbows inform my faith. It was my relationship with Hannah, God, and nature that caused me to look into the clouds, see a rainbow, and instantly know that Hannah's warm presence was near. As I thought about it, I realized I had been having experiences of God through nature and receiving messages through prayer for years. But these were so natural, I did not always pay special attention to them. My grief had raised my spiritual antenna to hear messages from the communion of saints.

According to Raymond Moody, in his book *Reunions,* medical research has shown that as many as 66 percent of widows see apparitions of their departed husbands. An apparition is distinct from a dream. In an apparition the living presence of the deceased person is vividly and unmistakably felt or sensed. Often seeing an apparition convinces a person that there is indeed life beyond death. For Christians, sensing such a "supernatural" presence is common. Christians often receive what they believe to be signs, callings, or visitations from angels. The Bible is full of these stories.

Life Beyond Death

The week after Hannah's death, I went into a bookstore. I was drawn to a table with books about angels. Something from my subconscious, or perhaps from another sphere, was leading me to purchase a book about angels. I felt a strong urge to look at the book, yet I felt a great deal of resistance to purchasing the book. I had been curious about the popularity of books and conferences on angels as a sociologist is curious about a new social behavior. I had believed that there was probably some truth as well as some illusion in the popular notions of angels. As a pastor, I had been afraid to speculate on the phenomena. With the rising popularity of angels, the church has not given guidance through warning and affirmation. There is a fear, when we move from stating that there is life after death to describing what that life might be like, that our speculation could be wrong, and we might mislead others. It was through opening the door to possibilities of thinking about the afterlife that I found comfort and powerful affirmations of life and faith.

It was this open door that caused me to buy the angel book. I read only five or six stories of miraculous rescues before I had to put the book down. My imagination didn't need any more feeding. My reading also raised the painful question, If angels protect and help some people, why not all? If angels are involved in human affairs, are their abilities limited? It would surely be cruel for some people to be saved and for others to perish. These questions ran through my mind. I was frantically swimming in questions, trying to find something to hold on to for security.

When I was young and before I had experienced much loss or pain, I told friends that I was not sure I believed in life after death. If there was life beyond death, I reasoned, it will be a wonderful grace, but if not, it doesn't lessen the Christian gospel for me. This statement was in response to a faith based on what we used to jokingly call "fire insurance." Some ministers attempted to scare the "hell" out of parishioners, and I didn't want to come to God out of fear. That to me, seemed disgraceful rather than graceful.

I was greatly influenced by the social gospel, which taught that the important issues in our lives were how we treated one another, and how we helped to create a better, more loving earth. This mission was the fulfillment of God's call. At a young age, I thought I knew everything and was in control of my faith and world. Only after disappointments, grief, and hurt did I begin to find hope in the Christian belief of life after death.

It was after Kelly had a miscarriage that I seriously began to wrestle with the importance of an afterlife. I was greatly grieved at this loss and thought of my parents, who were both deceased, playing with this tiny grandchild in heaven. I prayed for them to care for this child we would not get to know. I wrote a lament, which reveals my honest hopes for the afterlife. Here is one revealing passage:

> If the story of heaven is true
> and upon the shore, we land.
> Will our child greet us
> Singing songs of holy sands?

It is interesting to me that in the two times I have faced the death of a child, I moved from cognitive, clinical "weighing the facts about heaven" to a posture of clinging to the hope of life after death. It leads me to believe that not far from the surface, I held the belief or hope in the existence of angels and the afterlife all along. In facing these traumas, I needed the help of the communion of saints and God's messengers—the angels. Once I opened the door to the possibility of the work of angels and spirits connecting earth and heaven, then I began to experience the comfort, guidance, and support from realms other than earthly. This should not have been a surprise, for I had tapped into this spiritual energy source many times during my lifetime, but never with such trust and reliance—and response.

The skeptical side of my personality has doubted and pondered whether my mind had just improvised this idea to give me comfort and fulfilled a wish to relieve my pain. After all, when we are dealing with mysteries, we are simply speculating and can prove nothing.

Raymond Moody has done extensive research with people who have had near-death experiences. There are similarities that cross cultural and economic boundaries. We have all heard of these findings—a tunnel, a bright light, and a peaceful experience of love. And often in individuals who have such experiences, a transformation occurs that leads them to spend more energy caring for others and expressing love to those around them. Dr. Moody says that after all these years of work in the field he can't prove that there is another realm beyond the human realm of existence. He doesn't know if there are angels, or if in the mysteries of our brain there is a source of knowledge that moves into action at the time of death. He simply reports what different persons claim to experience and tries to draw some possible conclusions from their reports.

Each night I sang to Hannah and Sarah, "All night, all day, angels watching over you, my Lord . . . " What does it mean to sing and believe the message of this song? I could only hope that the angels helped Hannah cross over to the next world. What does it mean to say in the Apostles' Creed, "I believe in the communion of saints"? As a minister, I felt I should know about these things, but I didn't. But after Hannah's death, I began to take seriously the Christian teaching of everlasting life.

It is quite normal to worry about and think about what a loved one is doing after their death. They were a part of your life and will continue to be a part of your life. "What are you doing?" was a constant question I asked of Hannah after her death. When returning to her grave alone, I sat down and asked the question over and over again. I did not get an answer. I went to my parents' grave and prayed for them to take care of Hannah.

I have recounted Kelly's vivid dream the night after the tornado. In the dream, as she was pulling concrete blocks and bricks off of people, she noticed a bright place toward the altar of the church where happy children were playing. This to her was a vision of heaven, and it gave her great comfort. When we learned some time later that persons who have had near-death experiences often describe colors more brilliant than they have ever seen, this gave Kelly some affirmation that perhaps what she saw was true.

As he lay on the ground outside the sanctuary, one woman recognized her husband by the unique ring he wore. Other people remember the ring being on his finger. She asked about the ring at the funeral home and they did not know anything about the ring. Several days later, after she questioned many people, she found the ring on her husband's night stand beside their bed. She asked if someone had placed it there, but no one has confessed to ever touching the ring. Could her husband's spirit have the angelic power to move the ring and place it on the bedside table, where only they knew he ordinarily placed it each night?

The mother of a thirteen-year-old son who was crushed under the wall desired, as most grieving parents do, one last hug from her son. What grieving person hasn't longed and pleaded with God for one more visit with their loved one? This mother shared with me that during the night after the tornado she had the most vivid dream she has ever had. Her son, who was unharmed and happy, came to her, and she gave him a long hug. When she was ready to let go, he told her he had to go. She said, "I know." And he left. She immediately awoke from this dream or vision, with the assurance that her son was okay; she had been given the gift of closure she wanted.

When the tornado blew out the window next to her in the sanctuary, Diane Molock picked up her three-year-old nephew, Tyler, and laid herself on top of him in the aisle. Diane was killed, but her nephew survived. Tyler's mother, Lisa, has sensed Diane's presence many times since her death. When the Goshen church broke ground for the new church, children released helium-filled balloons to send to heaven for their friends who had died. Upon returning to his seat, Tyler told his mother that he had sent a yellow one to "Dine." Diane had given Tyler his first pacifier, and Lisa had not seen it for years. One day when Lisa opened the closet door, she looked down, and at her feet was that first pacifier. Lisa was immediately aware of Diane's presence.

Where does this "presence" come from? Is it projected from the depths of our memories? Does it come from the spirit of the dead to our spirit through our memories? The next illustrations lead me to believe that the spirit world can come to speak to us from outside of ourselves.

About three months after Diane's death, Diane's mother was sad because she did not get to tell her daughter goodbye. During the night, she awoke and saw Diane's face with a glow around it. They communicated not with words but with thoughts. Diane's mother just wanted to tell her that she loved her one more time and to say goodbye. Diane asked about her nephew Tyler. Diane's mother wanted to make sure this was not a dream and looked over at the clock and saw that it was four o'clock. When she looked back to where Diane's face had appeared, it had disappeared. But she was filled with the knowledge and comfort that Diane was okay.

Mary Woods's husband and daughter were killed in the tornado. Mary was seriously injured. After months of not sleeping well, she was greatly depressed. She awoke in the night, and at the foot of her bed was a bright, shining presence. It gave her warmth and comfort. Mary knew that this was God's presence. She communicated with this ball of light through thoughts. It told her to rest, and gave her the assurance that everything would be okay. Mary took in the warmth and was able to sleep more soundly than she had in months. The vision gave her hope and comfort to go on.

Since I became open to the possibility of the communion of saints ministering to us as angels and messengers, a whole new world has opened up to me in prayer and awareness. Time after time persons in our community have shared their experiences of the comforting presence of God and their loved ones who had been killed visiting them in some form. It has happened to Kelly and me many times. In preparing this book, I was writing in a quiet, still home, and Hannah's booster seat strap fell to the floor. I was aware of her presence. I cannot prove any feeling I have, it is simply an awareness.

One of the best illustrations of Hannah helping me was when we were designing the Hannah Clem playground at Camp Sumatanga. Kelly and I had picked out playground equipment we thought Hannah would enjoy, but we were still uncertain about where to place the playground. The camp trustees had planned for a small playground near a new building. We thought we would fit this playground into their plan. But there were several problems with this location and with the time frame I felt so compelled to keep. I was driven to have the playground completed and dedicated on Easter Sunday 1995 as a symbol of something good coming out of the destruction. I talked with the architect who was designing the new building, and he was trying to work with the location we talked about. The problems were enormous. I hung up knowing that something was wrong with the plan.

I did not know what to do. I felt so strongly that we could have the playground completed. I felt as if I were on a spiritual crusade to make this happen, and something was holding it up.

I did what I sometimes do when I need guidance from God: I took a nap, asking for God to speak to me through my dreams and subconscious. I awoke from my twenty-minute nap with an overwhelming confidence that the playground needed to be built in a new location. I called the architect, and he thought the new location could work. He agreed to meet me at Camp Sumatanga the next morning, before I met with the camp trustees to determine the site. The next morning, I sat on the new site. It was much better than I had ever imagined. I sat beside the lake and called for Hannah's help. I asked her where she wanted this playground to be located. I heard her clearly say, in my thoughts, "You already know where it's gonna go, you silly daddy. Who do you think helped you choose that place yesterday?" I was overjoyed and overwhelmed that Hannah had perhaps caused my uneasiness, and given some guidance in where it needed to go through my sleep. I met with the board, and they graciously approved the plans and location. The playground is located in a wooded area that provides shade and a great view of the lake. When I had thought of placing a playground, I thought we needed an open field. But through this vision or message, I awoke convinced that this location was right.

After I began having these experiences and hearing from others who were having similar experiences, I remembered Sarah's simple faith that her sister is still alive. Developmental psychologists say that she believes her sister is alive because of her childish reasoning. "She will grow out of it," they say. I hope she doesn't, and I hope that I am able to return to a simple faith that believes that Hannah and all others are alive, continuing to grow and develop in their journey of grace.

Sarah and Hannah had a Barbie beanbag chair, which they destroyed right before the tornado. In Sarah's mind, the beanbag chair's disappearance occurred at the same time many of her toys disappeared because of the tornado. Sarah has figured out that Hannah and Amy Woods get to sleep on this Barbie beanbag chair. After hearing Sarah talk about this beanbag chair for a while, we broke down and got Sarah another.

In looking at her books, Sarah held up one of the books that she knew was Hannah's and said, "Here Hannah, you take your book." Sarah has the faith to think that Hannah sees her and hears her. She will take something special and hold it up for Hannah to see. "What are you doing?" I'll ask. She responds, "Showing it to Hannah." In her mind, Hannah is alive. When Sarah swings, she tries to swing high to the sky so that in a way she is playing with Hannah. She wanted to hike with me up a mountain because she wanted to be closer to Hannah, who is alive in the sky with God.

When we dedicated the playground, the bishop said that he thought Hannah was present with us, climbing as high as she could, still with her great sense of adventure and with her wonderful smile. As he spoke, the eyes of Hannah's young friends grew wide, and they looked over at the playground with the hope of seeing Hannah swinging and climbing. Many of our friends told us they sensed her presence on the playground that day.

When we sense the presence of one who is beyond the grave, we have a communion that is more intimate than communication. It is a mystery to me what part of the "spirit" takes part in this communion. The communion is full of memories, and when we remember and think of the other, it keeps the communion alive. How sad it would be if the communion were only one-sided. Through the experiences I have described above, the communion with our loved ones is not one-sided, but our loved ones have chosen to make their presence known to us just as we have longed for them.

The Eucharistic prayer now has more meaning for me as I think of Hannah, my parents and grandparents, and other saints joining us for the celebration. "And so, with your people on earth and all the company of heaven we praise your name and join their unending hymn: Holy, holy, holy Lord, God of power and might, heaven and earth are full of your glory. Hosanna in the highest. Blessed is he who comes in the name of the Lord. Hosanna in the highest."

When I pray for the help of the saints to complete a task, I believe I am releasing the energy of God's love to actually guide me and help me do something. In *After Death,* Leslie Weatherhead writes that "Prayer is an act of faith in God's love. We release his power into other lives—even after death."

A wise friend has said that one of the greatest assets of the Goshen United Methodist Church is the communion of saints. We may call them angels, guides, or an extension of God's spirit, but I readily acknowledge a mysterious power that gives insights and messages to those who take the step to listen and make sacred a space to receive. I call these gifts one more extension of God's grace.

Leslie Weatherhead uses the image of the football game as one way to describe how the communion of saints are spectators of our lives. They watch and cheers us on. We are playing on a field and can feel the presence of those saints who are hoping we will make good decisions as we play the game. They see with larger eyes than human eyes, but that doesn't mean they see with godly eyes—for they are not God. In being closer to such goodness and light, they see their own shortcomings and realize they have different tasks than they had on earth. We bring them both pleasure and pain, just as we bring God both pleasure and pain.

A young Jewish reporter told us that the concept of life after death and the resurrection was totally new to her. "You seem to gain comfort in this idea," she said. It was true. In pondering the alternative, I realized that this belief was really so much a part of me that it was assumed. A professor once told me that we find out what we really believe not from presenting ideas on theological topics, but by living through crisis. As William Cummings said, "There are no atheists in the foxholes." In this crisis, I found a great deal of comfort in the few words Jesus did say about life after death. Perhaps it was so much a part of his life that he took it for granted. In John's Gospel, Jesus says, "Do not let your hearts be troubled. . . . In my Father's house there are many dwelling places. If it were not so, would I have told you that I go to prepare a place for you?" (John 14:1-2).

Dying on the cross, Jesus says to the thief, "Today you will be with me in Paradise" (Luke 23:43).

To his friend Martha Jesus says, "I am the resurrection and the life. Those who believe in me, even though they die, will live" (John 11:25).

These statements about life after death are very direct. I do not believe in life after death because of the near-death experiences recorded in Dr. Moody's book. They do give me comfort and a greater understanding of possibilities. Although it is convincing, I do not believe in life after death because I have known Hannah's presence in a variety of ways since her death. I cherish these moments, as well as the stories others have shared about their visions and sacred memories, but even without them, I would believe in life after death because I follow Jesus, who said that it was true.

Returning to Piedmont

"Today, my first goal is to find a place to live," I noncha-
lantly announced to my secretary. She stared at me for a
moment, then turned away, shaking her head. I badly
wanted a quick fix, but the expression on my secretary's face
reminded me that everything had changed in the past two
weeks. Perhaps my voice announcing my goal of finding
shelter was the same voice I used to tell her I was going to
the post office. My appearance was probably normal. Nor-
malcy was everyone's hope, especially mine, but "normal"
was no longer in our vocabulary.

Normally, a United Methodist church is responsible for
providing housing for its clergy family, but after the tornado
blew the roof off the church, only one person on the parson-
age committee could walk. Only three trustees could walk.
The congregation was too injured and battered to begin to
carry the load of caring for their pastor's family. They needed
Kelly to care for them. Everyone, including us, needed more
care than we could have imagined. I am not sure this is an
accurate picture, but it was our perception at the time. I felt
it was up to us and the volunteers we helped coordinate to
find us a home and get settled. Fortunately, volunteers came
to help!

With the large number of families seeking shelter, we felt
fortunate when a fellow United Methodist pastor offered to
allow us to stay in a home he had recently purchased. The
house had not been occupied for several years and was badly
in need of repair. I called friends in the construction business

to find some good painters; and a small company, a husband and wife, looked over the house and agreed to start painting the next day. The house was fully stocked with the previous owner's belongings, and these had to be packed and moved. Volunteers and the previous owner came to help. Kelly and I put our energy into cleaning and fixing up the house. The house had a patio with a great view of a mountain range to the east. Dogwoods bloomed in the yard, and we knew the house would be a great refuge for the time being.

We stayed busy picking out carpet and light fixtures and working with volunteers, as well as trying to deal with the slow but intense energy of grief. I felt as if I were moving with a bubble or a cloud around my head. Sometimes it was a cloak of grace, sometimes a storm cloud. One minute I could be full of peace and the next full of fury. We made daily trips to the post office to receive our boxes of mail. The post office was willing to let us carry home the boxes of mail in their large crates. We had stacks of crates in my office at the Wesley Foundation, at the district superintendent's house, and in the home where we were moving. Occasionally we would open a package or some letters. A Unity church sent Sarah a talking teddy bear with cassette tapes of calming stories and songs. A bank sent a box of teddy bears to be given to the surviving children for Easter. Huge poster boards with signatures of people who were praying for us poured in. We rented the last available storage building in Piedmont. Reporters continued to come daily to check on our progress. Volunteers were calling and wanting to bring work teams to help build homes and rebuild the church.

An eighteen-wheel tractor trailer from Charlotte, North Carolina, pulled into the church parking lot. United Method-ists had collected clothing, furniture, toys, and lumber to be given to the church. The proud people of Goshen said, "There are others in the community who need it more than we do." The volunteers from North Carolina insisted that it be used for church members first. The word spread about the load from the caring folks in North Carolina. Families went through the donated materials and picked out what they needed. Many were like us and didn't want to accept charity, but since it was given just for us, we would at least consider it. Kelly chose some toys for Sarah, including a rocking horse. We put the horse in our new house, and Sarah bounced and bounced on her new toy. She begged to stay at her new house with her rocking horse and stuffed animals. I looked through the furniture and picked out a desk, a stuffed chair, a sofa, and a few beds. Friends from the church helped bring the furniture to the new house. Kelly and I both had the feeling that this would be all we needed for a new home. Several nights later, when the painters finished and after the Piedmont Lion's Club gave us some sheets and towels, we spent our first night in our new home. Sheets hung from the bedroom windows those first weeks before a volunteer put up some miniblinds. The next morning I took a shower with no shower curtain. I wanted to make a cup of coffee, but we had no pots, cups, or microwave. I felt so silly being angry at our dependence upon such things as microwaves and shower curtains. We ate at McDonald's for breakfast, again. Piedmont has very few restaurants, and eating out had become old.

That day I went by the Disaster Relief Center for the first time. I was hoping for a shower curtain, silverware, and a vacuum cleaner, or perhaps a coffeepot. They didn't have the supplies I was wanting. I felt odd and out of place. I still did not want to take charity, but the workers insisted that I take some food and diapers. That night I was hungry and had a headache. Kelly was away for a meeting, and I wanted to cook something. I still had no pots or pans, but I decided I could open a can of pork and beans and a box of crackers. To my great frustration, I could not find a can opener. I had many cans of food but no can opener. I lost it. When Kelly came home, I immediately went to the store and bought a can opener. My tantrum embarrassed me a few days later when, behind a box, I found a can opener.

My emotions were like a bouncing ball. One bounce was anger, another bounce was self-pity. The next was guilt, knowing others were worse off than we were. The ball would bounce and shake me into pride, thinking I was strong and able to handle the situation well. I would gloat in this state until the next bounce threw me into fits of anger and depression that we were in this situation in the first place. The moments of depression dragged me down. I would sit listlessly. Then something would happen to cause me to bounce up and function positively. I knew many people worse off than we were; and I felt guilty for whining or complaining. But I couldn't help it—I whined and complained anyway. It was as if I couldn't control myself. The ball was moving and landing randomly at different levels of emotion. I felt the shame of complaining, but it also felt good. I wondered if it were my wounded pride that kept me from enjoying the release of complaining. My awareness of our neighbors' and friends' terrible losses caused me to downplay our own losses. But as much as I tried, I could not push down the pain. While our belongings were in boxes and would eventually be returned, our friends' belongings were strewn through fields and woods for miles, even into Georgia. Many of our friends were still suffering in the hospital. I felt guilty for complaining because I didn't have a microwave or a vacuum cleaner. Maya Angelou wrote about the simultaneous feelings of guilt and joy in her book, *I Know Why the Caged Bird Sings*. As a young girl, Angelou is sitting on the front row during a long church service and can't control her bladder. In desperation, she runs down the center aisle, releasing her urine. She is humiliated and yet feels the exuberance of release. Like Angelou as a young girl, I could handle frustrations and pain and inconvenience for only so long. Then I would simultaneously feel the exuberance, guilt, and shame of releasing my anger.

I kept being drawn back to the rubble. Each day I would have to spend some time just looking through the bricks and blocks. I was looking for something, but I wasn't sure what. Did the rubble hold some missing pieces to the puzzle of what happened? Each day as I looked, a constant flow of visitors turned into the driveway to come and look. I encouraged some to take bricks as a remembrance of the church. Many brought money and handed me checks. One day as I was looking, I found my baby book wrapped in a plastic bag, just as my mother had kept it years ago. I grabbed it up. To my amazement, the pages and pictures were moist but not soggy. I showed everyone who came that day. I said, "I found my baby book in the rubble of the church." I was as excited as if I had discovered a buried treasure.

Reading the laments in the Psalms helped me understand how easily exaggeration comes to those in pain. Psalm 22 is a lament that expresses the writer's feeling of abandonment by God. The psalmist writes that wild animals such as the bulls of Bashan, dogs, and lions surround him with open mouths. Is this an exaggeration? When the psalmist describes his heart melting like wax and all his bones slipping out of joint, perhaps his feeling is real even if these things are not literally happening. Such pain is hard to understand or describe. Perhaps the psalmist and I weren't exaggerating our pain, but finding that an adequate description was impossible.

Kelly was in her own world of organizing volunteers, doing interviews, and caring for the congregation. I called her a bulldog, because she kept working so hard for such long hours. She could not stop to sleep. Just watching her made me tired, as she pushed herself—talking on the phone, answering questions, and doing interviews with the media. I wrote in my journal, "Kelly's 'heroine' is working overtime, and pretty soon she will collapse." I worried about establishing a home, and she worried about caring for others. Over a period of a few months, volunteers washed windows, replaced door knobs, cut the grass, put up molding, replaced bad wiring, changed light fixtures, hung miniblinds, and made Sarah some Aladdin curtains to match her Aladdin sheets and comforter.

It took a great deal of time to replace items lost in the tornado. A Sunday school class of First United Methodist in Jacksonville put a swing set together for Sarah. I learned to try to buy preassembled floor models of items I was replacing so I wouldn't have to put them together. I was much too frazzled to have the patience to put a gas grill or patio furniture together.

The phone continued to ring with callers wanting to bring work teams, sell us something, send money to help, or ask if we had received their letters.

There were touching visits from friends and strangers who drove to Piedmont to give us a hug and perhaps a check. One retired couple from Ashland followed the story in the news and drove to Goshen. They saw the destroyed site and stopped at Abbott's Place, a local gas station, wanting to find us. A church member was working at the station and agreed to take them to our house. I had just arrived when they pulled up and parked among the painters' trucks. The well-dressed man and woman introduced themselves as United Methodists and the parents of a professor I knew. The woman told me that she had experienced something of a supernatural call to come and give us a gift from Hannah. When she said this, I felt my heart leap and begin to beat rapidly. She said, "I know this may sound strange, but I really feel that Hannah wanted me to give you a gift. She and we would like for you to have something special—a meal out, a new dress for Kelly—anything special." She made out the check and on the bottom wrote, "from Hannah." We both cried as we hugged goodbye.

We had volunteers to help us organize our kitchen, clean the house, send thank-you notes, open the mail, and work in the yard. Kelly asked a friend to begin a database of the memorial donations received for Hannah's playground.

Kelly's pastoral responsibilities were overwhelming. She writes:

> At first, everyone required a long conversation. All the givens in our church were replaced by uncertainties. It was days before we knew who was injured, where they were, and what their conditions were. It was months before the story of what happened finally came together. Each conversation involved many questions. Simple answers did not seem like honest answers. The polite replies "I'm fine, and you?" would have been a joke. Basic questions such as "How are your kids?" were replaced by "Have your kids slept in their own room yet?" or "What are you doing with your ruined furniture?"

"Where can I hug you?" was a common question exchanged among church members. So many times, people—especially strangers—felt compelled to hug tightly without being aware that these bodies were sore and had suffered a trauma. The embraces were tolerated, but among those who had survived the tornado, we knew one another's need to be embraced without suffering further injuries.

The grief made Kelly's job nearly impossible. She reflects:

> Ministering to a congregation with this much devastation was impossible. It was like standing on the edge of many desolate, dry, grand canyons created by falling meteors a mile wide. I was on the edge of these craters, looking at destruction as far as I could see. One crater at a time, I would look down into the crater, take a breath, and say a prayer to gather my energy to start the descent. Down I would climb to be with another person in grief. I arrived with my external wounds, black eyes, and an injured shoulder, as well as a broken heart. With each climb into another's grief space, my strength left me. I made the climb simply to share the grief, offer a prayer, and try to plant seeds of hope. The more trips I made into the craters, the easier the paths and climbs became.

The craters I saw were not just those of my congregation and family, but of all those who were suffering from shock and grief. That included the extended family of our congregation and their friends. It included counselors, pastors, police officers, and rescue workers. It even included the reporters who covered the tragedy. All seemed to look to me for guidance, strength and grace.

Grief doesn't follow a timetable, and I don't think there is any way to grieve for more than one person at a time. At a workshop in Gadsden I asked Hanna Schock, a friend who had lost her two sisters and mother in a car accident, "How do you grieve for more than one?" She responded that each loss must be dealt with separately. So one day I would grieve for the loss of Hannah by entering that crater. The next, I might enter the craters and space of the Mode family and pray for their three-year-old son Zachary, who died, and the children who survived. One by one I would take those who died and enter into those craters and the craters of their family members. I could only grieve for them separately. It was impossible to do it all at once. I would enter the crater and try not to avoid the sorrow and anger that accompanies the descent and ascent.

I grieved about my physical limits of not being able to use my right arm. I grieved for Sarah and her loss of her sister, friend, and guide. I grieved the loss of the playground where Sarah and Hannah played. Each of these griefs was a separate crater in a desolate desert landscape. Theologian Henri Nouwen writes that pastors stand on the edges of people's lives when significant events occur. We are invited to graduation parties by family members and to wedding rehearsals where toasts are offered. We stand with families at the birth of a child and on the edge of the grave. The tornado caused me to stand on the edges of many people's lives during major trauma, while in the midst of grief and trauma myself.

I tried to visit with one family a day. I thought if I could just visit one family a day, I would be doing well. But as it turned out, because of the chaos and emotional and physical survival demands, I sometimes was not able to make the visits. Each visit with a family lasted for hours. They cried for me and our loss of Hannah, and I cried for them. I think the visits were healing, but they drained us all. Often, I would leave a home and have to find a quiet place to rest. On more than one occasion, I went to a church member's home and took a nap. Once, while I was at a family's home, I noticed a large beach towel from Hawaii. It was being used by a thirteen-year-old boy who was staying at this home while his mother was recovering in the hospital. The towel came from our house. It was a gift from one of Dale's students who visited Hawaii. In the rescue efforts I had brought towels, sheets and blankets from our house to help treat for shock and give people something to wrap around their wet, injured bodies. I imagined the boy standing outside the rubble wrapped in this towel. I wanted to wrap my arms around him and give him some comfort, but the towel was all I had to offer. Only God can heal his broken heart. I hoped that this simple offering of a towel could bring a little bit of healing to him. It was the small acts of kindness that gave me the encouragement not to give up. As I visited other homes, I recognized other towels and blankets from our home. I doubted that anyone knew where these gifts came from. They came with the hopes and prayers of a brokenhearted pastor who wanted so badly to wrap a secure and warm blanket of love around a brokenhearted congregation on that tragic Sunday.

It was one of the first warm Saturdays of 1995. Sarah wanted to play outside as Kelly and I worked in the yard. Several of the dogwood trees in our yard were beginning to bloom. The two crabapple trees were in full bloom and looked like pink trees. When I saw how pink they were, I thought of the pictures of trees Hannah had drawn and colored pink. At the time I did not think that trees would ever be pink. The gentle breeze started blowing the soft, small, pink petals off the tree. Sarah sat on the ground under the

trees as the pink petals drifted down, transforming the ground from green and brown to pink. "It's snowing!" she exclaimed.

"Sweet sadness" is a paradoxical emotion, which the Japanese claim to be the best of emotions. Many Japanese families go each year to watch the cherry blossoms blow away from the trees. As I watched Sarah and the pink petals blowing, I thought of sweet sadness. Watching the yearly cycle of flowering blooms on trees seems natural and good. It is sad that the blooms must go, but I am able to understand that the blooming is a beautiful way of reproducing and survival. I know that next spring, the tree will probably bloom again. It is a simple and natural process. Human blooming and death does not seem so natural. It hurts too much to be natural. How could anything so painful be natural? Yet we all know that in the big picture of life, both life and death are natural and thus carry a sweet sadness.

Many experiences in life can be described as sweet sadness. When our girls learned to walk, we were excited that they were walking, but we missed the baby stage. The baby tooth falls out to make room for the permanent tooth. As our children grow into new stages, we love the new stage but miss the old stage. This transition is like those pink flower petals floating down around Sarah, giving her joy to imagine these magical blossoms of snow. It is a sweet sadness.

When one dies of a long, hard illness, the death is often seen as sweet sadness because we are glad the person is no longer suffering—but we miss the person just the same. While Kelly and I were in Africa, where death is common to all ages, we heard people speak of "crying with only one eye."

Survivors, Not Victims

While we were at Gulf Shores, Kelly was away from her pulpit at the church only one Sunday. On that particular Sunday, the congregation gathered inside a tent in the front yard of our old damaged home. The wind whipped the canvas tent back and forth. Loose flaps popped in the wind's current. The wind and noise scared the children and adults. The service concluded with more folks outside the tent than within. A local civic organization, the Oddfellows, offered the church the use of their lodge in Piedmont. Kelly's first Sunday worship service upon her return was held in the Oddfellows lodge.

In that worship service she asked the congregation, "What is a victim?" Someone said that a victim acts as though he or she can't do anything about his or her situation. Another offered, "A victim can't find a way out or won't take responsibility for their future."

Then Kelly asked, "What is a survivor?" Someone said, "A survivor endures and keeps going." Another added, "When knocked down, a survivor gets back up."

After their responses, Kelly discussed how victims act and how survivors act. She then paused and looked straight into the eyes of her congregation and said, "You don't look like victims to me. You look like survivors. The press keep calling us victims, but we are not helpless. God is helping us, and we keep living. God is helping us pull ourselves up in the midst of a terrible tragedy. You are not victims, but you are survivors. You are amazing!"

Several camera crews from Atlanta were in worship that day, as well as a photographer from *People* magazine. The photographer had spent several days in our midst and was sincere as he told Kelly that the service had really made an impact on his life. At that same worship service, one man approached several church members saying, "I want the faith that you have."

Doubting

On that same day, I preached at Jacksonville First United Methodist Church. I told the pastor, "I need to preach, because I have a fear that I can't preach anymore." I needed to preach but thought, "What can I possibly say after what has happened to us?" The scripture text in the lectionary that Sunday was Matthew 28:16-20, in which Jesus appears to the disciples after his death and resurrection. The disciples follow him to the mountain where some worshiped Jesus and some disciples doubted. I had never noticed that even while Jesus was in their midst, some doubted. The title of my sermon was, "What about the doubters?" It seemed very logical to me that disciples who had experienced an emotional roller coaster and who were in the midst of their own experience of numbing grief doubted that Jesus truly appeared to them. The amazing part of the story is that Jesus loved them and accepted them even in their doubts. Not only does Jesus accept them, but he sends them out to make disciples and observe the teachings of love and sacrifice. Jesus sends them out even when they are not sure what they believe. God was certainly empowering Kelly and me and members of the Goshen church to attempt to live a life of love, giving, and prayer, even with our grief and the doubts and confusion that came with them. Even in our doubts and confusion caused by grief, God can send each of us out to live a life of love, giving, and prayer. We were acting in a drama in which we somehow found hope and love even in the midst of great grief.

The Struggle with Ego

One day a young minister friend asked me, "How is this tragedy going to affect your ministry?"

I stuttered, and then I heard myself talking about how the sudden media attention could change our ministries and lives more than the tornado. Later I realized how my ego was being fed by the attention we received. I incorrectly correlated Hannah's life and my self-worth with this attention. Grieving persons often compare the response they receive with the response to others in similar situations. We say, "There were thirty visitors at the funeral home," as if the number of visitors, cards, or flower arrangements were an apt measure of the worth of the person who died. Such comparisons are not apt. Every life is of value!

When my friend asked me how this disaster would affect my ministry, it dawned on me that I needed to question my inner motivations. We had turned down several requests for interviews, invitations to appear on talk shows, and everyone who even mentioned movie rights. However, the ego is a tricky monster, which demands to be fed. Death robs the ego of self-esteem and confidence. I realized that if we were not careful, we could use the spotlight to feed a starved ego. If I let my ego go unchecked, I could lose my relationship with Kelly and perhaps my job. I hoped that we weren't traveling to California to appear on the talk show to meet our own ego needs, but to witness to God's grace. However, in this stage of grief, it is difficult to distinguish internal motives. These doubts were frightening and caused me to break out in a sweat.

The Struggle with Identity

Several years ago, author Sue Monk Kidd led a spiritual retreat Kelly and I attended and challenged us to keep searching for our identity. She asked if we would be the same—deep down—if we had a different family, spoke another language, lived in another country, and had a different vocation. This provocative question has helped me realize that my identity is not just shaped by the circumstances of life, but my identity is shaped from the depths of my soul by factors of which I am mostly unaware.

If I were to depict my life as a musical score, the period around Hannah's death would have notes, rests, and other musical markings falling off the page. The sound I enjoy imagining for this fall is the sound of a piano crashing after falling from a tall building. Grief has given me the opportunity to try to place the notes and rests back on the score. But the music that is now created will look and sound differently than it did before the piano crashed.

After I had spent thirty-four years trying to discover and define who I was, it was a challenge to be forced to pick up those notes once more and try to make music. The surprise is that at the depths of who I am, there are more songs and tunes than I ever imagined.

The hardest thing about searching for one's identity is honesty. We love our illusions about ourselves. The arts have helped me to see myself more clearly and honestly. I am shocked to see myself in the bizarre characters of Flannery O'Connor, or in the searching Tom Wingo in Pat Conroy's *The Prince of Tides*, or in the whisky priest in Graham Greene's *The Power and the Glory*, but I do. The humanity of the characters in the Bible is refreshing for me in a culture that seems to pressure us to only fall in line and reveal our positive attributes, muffling our dissonant chords. The Bible helps me to see myself honestly. Observing nature is a natural way for me to search and ask questions of myself. This search and probing is a way of prayer, and it gives me an opportunity to sit and listen, explore and create. The mystery of who we are is more complex than at first we can imagine.

Our Support Group

Kelly, the district superintendent, and others had invited anyone affected by the tornado to learn about possible support groups. We gathered at the Oddfellows lodge, where the Goshen church was worshiping.

It was an emotional gathering. Everyone seemed uncomfortable. The director of pastoral counseling for our North Alabama Conference led the meeting. I remember only a few important things being done at this initial meeting. We began by singing a hymn of faith.

The air was thick with tension. The people from Goshen looked as though they were in a pit of despair. I wondered if a group suffering with so much pain had ever gathered in one place. Counselors were introduced who would travel the journey with us. The pastoral counselor held up a handmade poster identifying three stages of disaster:

1. Emergency (two days)
2. Relief (lasts ten times longer than stage one) (twenty days)
3. Recovery (lasts ten times longer than stage two)
    (two hundred days)

As he explained the stages and their time spans, my mind raced ahead. I had trouble understanding his words. I tried to figure out whether the emergency had lasted two days or more. To me, the emergency seemed as if it had continued for a solid week. Two hundred days to recover seemed like a very long time. We were looking into December before we would be on the other side of the mountain. Someone also had told me that the hardest time would be in four or five months (in August). The long recovery period seemed ominous.

One of the counselors took a group member's wheelchair and placed it at one end of the room. I guess he thought that the sitting person would not need the wheelchair for the exercise. At the opposite end of the room, the altar table held a cross. The counselor explained that he wanted all of us who had gathered to think of the distance between the wheelchair and the altar as a measuring stick of healing and to place ourselves where we thought we were in the healing process. The wheelchair marked the beginning of the healing journey, and the altar marked recovery.

I stood behind the wheelchair. So much was out of control in my life. I felt I wasn't able to begin the road to recovery at that point in time. When I became a little more stable, I could move up to the wheelchair. I was glad the counselors asked us to respond and make a statement about ourselves through such a simple exercise. I assumed others were like me and wanted to talk.

People on crutches struggled to position themselves. People in wheelchairs rolled around, looking for their place in the continuum. A basic look of confusion was on the faces of most of us. I watched people try to determine where they would go. I wondered if people who gave the appearance of not being affected would walk up close to the cross, indicating that they were fine. It was a dilemma. If a person did actually think he or she was doing well, then did it dishonor a person like me, who felt out of control? At that point, we had not achieved a level of intimacy that allowed us to admit vulnerability. Later we learned to say, "Today I'm doing well," or "Today I'm not doing well," emphasizing that our grief and healing changed from day to day.

Our group struggled. It was obvious that some did not like the exercise. I was ready to yell, "I'm not well!" Some people stood in the middle and said that they thought they were doing fine. The majority stood close to the wheelchair and said that they thought they had a long way to go toward healing.

The second meeting of the support group did not have the tense atmosphere of the first. The meeting officially began when the door was closed and a prayer was said, but it had actually begun long before. It had begun during the week when someone, moved to tears thinking about the death of an uncle and cousins, had contemplated sharing her grief with the group. The meeting had begun in the cemetery, as a person had placed flowers on a grave and contemplated life after death. The meeting had begun two nights before, when a windy storm had whipped through the community, driving frightened families to sleep in hall closets, newly dug storm shelters, and bathrooms. The meeting had begun with these experiences, for in the circle these experiences would be thought about and perhaps shared.

Over the next few months, the meetings began as the circle was set and hugs and greetings exchanged. The meeting began as crutches, walkers, and wheelchairs were adjusted and pillows passed out to soften the feel of the hard metal folding chairs. Funeral home fans, with a blurry print of W. Sallman's portrait of Jesus on one side and an advertisement for the funeral home on the other, were distributed. Some people needed two fans or two pillows. These idiosyncrasies became part of the group's natural sense of humor and its rhythm of breaking the ice. This group loved to laugh, and took any opportunity to poke fun at one another. Humor had an important place in the support group. We often laughed at silly things, and group members enjoyed entertaining us with silly tales.

The spoken rules of the group included confidentiality and a desire for members who had urgent, burning issues to speak up and tell the group at the beginning of the session, so that the group would know how best to spend its energy and time. Diversity of opinion was expected and accepted.

The unspoken rules were just as important as the spoken rules. No one person was to dominate the group's time or to tell every story that came to mind as another person shared. Interrupting was as unacceptable as crying was accepted. Not only was crying acceptable, it was affirmed as the natural and appropriate emotion for anyone who had been through what everyone in the group had experienced. Preaching to one another was frowned upon. However, honestly sharing beliefs and feelings was encouraged, as long as polite respect was given someone who had a different perspective.

After some meetings, I left asking myself if it were worth my time. After other meetings, I left thinking that it was a privilege to be in the company of such friends sharing important parts of their lives. Sometimes my patience was low when the same questions were asked again and again, until the day I found myself asking the questions. My day did come, when questions screamed out in the night, echoed off the mountains, returning unanswered. How many times must we tell and hear our stories before our souls begin to heal? Nine times, nine times ninety? There is no magic potion to heal grief and suffering, for suffering is unique to each person, but there is something healing about sharing our common stories of pain, healing, and recovery.

Not everyone was present in the circle all the time, even though they were seated with us. Now and then I could look into the eyes of my friends and see that they were far away in some sacred space and time, reliving a memory, going over a conversation, or fighting a battle known only to them. Patience came to me when I thought of the burdens people carried.

Leaning Toward the Pain

Days after Hannah's funeral, I thought of Rilke's line, "The greatest gift you have to give the world, is your deepest burden." Fleshing out what it means and can mean for me has been a constant task during this year.

My neighbor, some twenty-five miles away, Dr. Raymond Moody, a psychologist and author, described to me his own grief experience. He drew a small circle within a larger one. He colored the small circle and called it a hole that represented his grief after losing a child. The larger circle represented his life. Over time, he said, the hole had never gone away, but his own life circle has expanded wider and wider.

This simple illustration fits my experience of the past year. It has been painful and difficult, but through the darkness, I have grown in unexpected ways and experienced new ripples of life. For me, moving toward the expanding circles describes the process whereby we are drawn out of ourselves and deeper into God's mystery and grace.

Kelly's and my experience so far has been that the emptiness and grief represented in that hole will be part of our lives forever. People have said to us, and I have said to others, that time heals grief. Yet after Hannah's death, I was angered when people said this to me. Years seem like a long time to wait for the pain to become bearable. During the year after the tornado, Kelly and I had periods of numbness, when we were shrouded with the grace of shock. We had other times when we plunged into deep despair. But throughout the year, the hole and emptiness in our lives remained constant. We continue to miss the daily, lively interaction with Hannah. To me, she will always remain four years old.

Grief is painful, hard stuff. How can you transform the hole into wholeness—into holiness? Transforming the hole into the holy is a very slow process.

There is a hole in my living room floor. The hole is like a volcano spewing hot, flaming gasses. How do we cool the fires of grief? For a while the hole acted as an anesthetic and numbed my whole body and house. But the anesthetic wore off, and the pain came. In the house of my life is a volcanic hole. The question now is this: "What do I do with this hole?"

The first option is to get some lumber and start stacking as many things as I can across the hole. Get a rug, some plants, and presto: No more hole! Each piece of lumber could be a task to keep myself busy and avoid the hole. Redecorating is a favorite activity of grieving persons, so a rug goes over the hole to make life livable.

I am not saying that staying busy is only negative. Having a role and a job can be the best thing for a grieving person. Setting achievable short-term goals is good for someone who is going through grief and crisis. In major disasters such as earthquakes and tornadoes, the people with specific roles to play function better in the long run than those who do not have specific roles.

I can't imagine someone losing a loved one without experiencing denial. The pain is too much to handle all at once. But the "hole in the living room floor" contains a great amount of steam that needs to be released safely and appropriately. We were so overwhelmed with trying to set up a new home, care for our family and others, and attend to the support mail that it took a while to find an appropriate outlet for those volcanic gasses. The way I expressed my pain was to write. I began to retreat to a borrowed trailer and write for hours about my experience.

If we do not pay attention to our grief, the volcanic steam will eventually start slipping through the cracks. More and more energy will be required to stop up the holes and keep in the steam. Instead of the steam being harnessed for positive productivity, the volcano will erupt in harmful ways—a hurtful comment or an explosion over a small, insignificant problem. The volcanic crater of grief will begin to eat away at our body. It grows, and we shrink. Before we know it, grief is controlling us rather than us controlling it. The pain of grief cannot be ignored forever.

I was blessed with opportunities to deal directly with my pain. I could pull a chair up beside the hole and simply get used to it. At first, only a minute or two was all I could stand. But with practice, the time I spent at the hole of pain increased. I would allow each wave of memory to rise and enter my body. I imagined myself embracing one painful memory or thought at a time. It took a great deal of time to allow these memories to come. My temptation was to rush around and avoid that living room with the hole altogether. Sometimes when a pain came from the hole I would run away, but eventually, I learned to imagine myself hugging the pain so hard that it became a part of my bones. Giving the painful wound my attention would exhaust my energy. But after a while I could imagine myself strapping on my rappelling gear and jumping in feet first. Eventually, the waves of pain came less often.

As I descended into the depths of my grief, I found many chambers that held cool, refreshing, healing waters. The process is ongoing. I am still on my journey through the hole, the caverns. I am trying to hug the pain so much that it becomes a part of my voice, my eyes, my life, my attitude.

Parker Palmer reminded me that the motto of the wilderness adventure organization Outward Bound is "If you can't get out of it, get into it." The only way to deal with the monsters is to move toward them, into them, and through them. In *The Active Life*, Palmer writes, "From the depths we can find the hidden wholeness that unites and energizes us, the source and power that makes us fully alive."

For those who grieve, I am convinced that the process of embracing the pain and learning to be nourished from the sources of pain will enable us to live with new depth, wisdom, and love.

The Emotions Go Deep

Men are said to have more trouble expressing their feelings than women. For months after the tornado, I had more feelings emerging than I could deal with. The stages of grief that Elisabeth Kübler-Ross identified are helpful because they give us names for what we may be experiencing. I have not found that the stages come in any particular order. The process of grief puts us in touch with more emotions than I wanted to acknowledge. The stages (*denial*—shock, confusion, asking what happened; *anger*—guilt, sadness, fear, depression; *bargaining*—looking for solutions, a cause, or a reason; and *acceptance*—letting go, learning, and moving on) involve a dance between mind and emotion. Healing must come from both aspects of our personalities. When I have been able to take the time to reflect upon my emotional gauge, I usually find that different parts of my personality feel different emotions, often conflicting emotions, at once. The question "How does it make you feel?" was such a popular cliché in seminary, we made up jokes and songs about it. When visiting patients in the hospital, I wondered if someone would look at me from his bed and yell, "You want to know how I feel? . . . How does this feel?" as he lunged forward and grabbed my throat with strong, big hands. My students have often made fun of my attempts to get them to probe their inner worlds and claim their emotions.

Although it is fun to ridicule and poke fun at counselors and pastors who try to help us examine our emotions, I believe that the emotions are an often untapped energy source for creativity, work, play, and vision. When we embrace and work with our emotions, they can enrich our lives and be the source of compassion and healing.

How does healing come after a loss? For me, healing has come as I have leaned toward the pain. The hole that causes so much pain is also the source of healing and wholeness. If I face the hole as best as I can and don't try to cover it up and ignore it, then healing comes. I get in trouble when I pretend the hole isn't there and try to live a "normal life" without giving the hole some attention.

Facing the pain is like planting a tree. At first it is work. You must dig the hole and get dirty. The tree needs respect, not only from you but from others. Your grief and emotions, like a newly planted tree, may need some stabilizing ties and stakes until they are strong. The neighborhood kids will have to be careful not to trample the tree when they play baseball or football in the yard. My next-door neighbors planted trees in their front yard each year, but the neighborhood games their boys organized destroyed the trees each year until the boys were out of college. A tree needs space to grow. It can't be covered up and smothered. It needs air to breathe in order to grow. The tree needs some stimulants such as water and fertilizer. The tree also needs something to give it warmth and light. I think of this as hope for the future. If there is no light of hope, there will be no growth. With patience and time, growth will occur with space, air, nurture, respect, and hope. But the growth will not mean the tree can be left untended. Growth occurs in the circles of our lives—like the circles of the tree. When the tree grows, it will offer shade and comfort.

We tend to block our emotions from our conscious awareness, especially if we don't approve of them. After a loss, sometimes we try to cut off our negative emotions—or all emotions. I tried to simply get back to work and deny my emotions. I learned that emotions can't be ignored. They are a part of who we are. I did not realize the connection between our minds and our bodies. We are multifaceted beings. Emotions affect our bodies, and our bodies affect our emotions. If we do not give our emotions the space and respect they need, they will let our bodies know something is wrong through illness, nervous breakdowns, affairs, acting out, and other signs of dysfunction.

Our emotions are a well of what is truly important—love, compassion, loyalty, pity, kindness. The water from this well feeds the soul of our community and world. The well also contains negative emotions that must be dealt with, such as jealousy, guilt, shame, envy, and hate.

I have always said and heard that God enters into our feelings and understands our joys, pains, and melancholy. God must have a large imagination to enter into the depths of the emotions of so many. Suffering is always personal and unique because we all have different histories. Suffering is different for each person, yet when one person shares his or her suffering, it has a mysterious effect upon others. If we allow the suffering of another to flow over us like water, the gentle flow may allow us to break down some of the protective walls we have erected to separate us from our own pain. The healing waters can cleanse us and leave us refreshed, realizing once again that we are truly human.

During the past few years, I have become aware of others who really did attempt to enter into our pain or their pain for us. Through sharing stories and using our imagination, we more clearly define who we are and what is important. We enrich our lives when we cultivate our appreciation of others.

What does it mean to enter into the emotions of another? Creation itself shows signs of the breadth of God's emotions. The intricate details of color in creation are glorious. The earth experiences destruction and chaos by fire, flood, earthquake, and wind. Yet over time, each season has its own beauty. Surely God, who created this small blue planet and the larger universe, expresses feelings in the universe that go deeper than we will ever imagine. We get a sense of God's feelings through the life of Jesus. In the story of the wedding feast at Cana, we see that Jesus enjoyed the company of friends and appreciated the importance of marking the time with celebrations. Jesus' crucifixion demonstrates God's way of entering into the pain and suffering of the world.

The imagination is deep, and when we allow ourselves the time and space to explore our feelings, then we are able to live life differently and at a deeper level. Through living life at a deeper level, we are able to relate to others in more caring and loving ways. Because of my experience of grief, I now empathize more deeply with others who are struck by tragedy. The stories come alive for me as I let my feelings well up from inside me and wash over me like waves. I have the possibility of lifting these persons up in prayer as I attempt to create a sacred space of hospitality where both their feelings and my own can exist.

Faith

What have I learned about faith during this year? Many people have asked me if I still believe that God never wills suffering on people. I must answer with the same belief that I did shortly after the tornado. I don't believe that God sends tornadoes to bring death and destruction to a community any more than God sent Hitler to Germany, communism to Cuba, or capitalism to the United States. God does not cause the rain forests to disappear. The natural laws that operate on this fragile blue ball we call home do not change because we want them too. Natural disasters are simply part of creation. Pain, suffering, and death are part of creation, just like joy, happiness, and hope.

Another question people have asked me concerns whether suffering occurs in our lives in order to teach us something. I do not believe that we can explain suffering. Must everything have a reason? I can't explain why the world is here in the first place. Should the fact that human beings become sick and move into the great mystery of death be any more mysterious than the question of why we were born in the first place? What we can say with some certainty is that death visits us all. Whether good or ill comes from suffering, suffering remains unexplainable. Václav Havel is right to encourage us to recognize that something more is going on in the world than can be explained, described, and controlled. In a 1992 lecture to the World Economic Forum, Havel said, "We have to abandon the arrogant belief that the world is merely a puzzle to be solved, . . . a body of information to be fed into a computer in the hope that, sooner or later, it will spit out a universal solution." What we do know is that we can live faithfully and have communion with God and one another. We know that God created all that is, and that God's love is expressed in the life of Jesus Christ, who died and was resurrected from the dead. We know that Jesus has experienced pain and suffering, and even questioned God.

Knowing these things can bring meaning to life, but it is a loving community who can absorb our pain and heal our grief.

I have chosen to use my experience to learn. The death of a child is not meaningful; it is simply painful and absurd. I could have just as easily chosen to be bitter and reject any love that God or anyone else offered me. But I have experienced a deeper appreciation of God's mystery and presence than I had before the tornado. I returned from the first year after Hannah's death not with a blueprint of God's actions but with a spirit filled with awe and wonder.

The circle of my experience of God has expanded. A saying that became very meaningful to many of us at Goshen was, "Sometimes God calms the storm, and sometimes God calms the child."

God never promised that the storms of life would be calmed, but God did promise that God's presence would never leave us; and we have felt God's powerful presence. In *The Spirituals and the Blues,* James Cone writes, "Because the faithful can experience the reality of divine presence, they can endure suffering and transform it into an event of redemption. An encounter with God is the ultimate answer to the question of faith, and it comes only in and through the struggle for righteousness—not in passivity."

Through the variety of ways I have experienced God during the past few years, my faith has remained solid and given me strength. Faith is not a set of beliefs or a blueprint of a great mystery. Any belief system can only tell part of the truth, for God's truth is beyond our imagination. Faith is a relationship with a companion. Faith is praying and being attentive to God all around us. Faith is screaming out your feelings of pain. Faith is searching, asking, and sometimes even wrestling with God. Faith is developing a tender and compassionate heart for others. Faith is asking for help. Faith is calling on the communion of saints for wisdom. Faith is accepting that you are special in God's sight. Faith is stepping into an unknown future, knowing that God is at your side, and that each step may be your last. Faith is a spirit, an attitude in which you live your life. Faith is knowing that you are part of a mysterious force that is bigger than this life. Faith is trusting that God will lead you into the great mystery we call death.

The Story Is About the Faith

Reporters have constantly asked us about our faith and about the role God played in the tornado; but as I have said before, we were interested in discussing the role God was playing in keeping us going.

A reporter said, "But the Bible says that 'all things work together for good, for those who love God.' " I had to respond that I remembered the passage to say, "In all things God works for the good . . . " (Romans 8:28 NIV). God doesn't will all things, but God works in all things to help bring good into the world.

For many of these reporters, the story went deeper than the average story—this story had shaken their faith. Even if they were not practicing Christians, they believed that churches should be safe and protected by God. The two main questions we were asked were, "Why do you think God would cause or allow such a disaster to happen to a church?" and, "Has this shattered your faith?" At the time, I had no idea how deeply these questions had taken hold of the world.

Asking why is not sacrilegious or unfaithful. It simply was not my question at the time. Jesus himself prayed the cry of Psalm 22 on the cross, "Why have you forsaken me?" The "Why" question is asked throughout our praying tradition. Dag Hammarskjøld was killed in a plane crash in Africa. His sister visited his grave and put on the grave marker the question, "Why?" Why must good brothers be killed in plane crashes? Why must children die of starvation? There is a sense that without answers people will simply go mad.

Many have asked me, "Could God have stopped the tornado?" and I have answered that God has set the world in motion and does not normally, to my knowledge, interfere with nature. It would be a strange world indeed if the laws of nature were constantly being changed to accommodate our desire to live. It would cause much chaos if God changed the laws of gravity if a bird fell out of its nest or a person fell off a cliff. Trucks that begin to hydroplane don't fly to keep from crashing. God does not stop the rain when we forget our umbrella.

A minister told me that my theology makes me an atheist, because the God I describe is weak and not active in human life. Kelly and I have consistently said that we have been upheld by God's grace before this tragedy, throughout this ordeal, and since. I have not experienced God as weak, but as strong and loving. I have expressed my hurt and rage to God in prayer. Obviously, I did not get what I wanted—I did not get my daughter back. This makes me angry, but not at God.

Others have accused me of trying to defend God. When I decided to make public statements about faith to the press, I was not trying to defend God as much as I was attempting to express my particular faith in God—which is different from the theology that believes God controls every situation. Perhaps I stand guilty of trying to defend my understanding of the way God works in the world (and the way God does not work in the world). In our interviews, Kelly and I never downplayed the absurdity of suffering and loss. What we attempted to do was dispel the oversimplified notion of God as puppeteer.

Faith to me is standing and believing in God, even when our lives don't make sense. Although some people find comfort in clichés and simple answers, I do not. Simply speaking of nature and God in rationalistic ways reduces

God to our level and takes away the mystery. For me, death is a wall that says *no*. The *no* is illogical and shatters what we wanted to believe about ourselves, God, and the world. We have spent much of our lives building a safe place where walls keep out dangers, and risks are kept to a minimum. We protect ourselves by our ideas about God and the world. For instance, we may believe that God loves us and will not allow anything bad to happen to us. In our own minds, we build this wall of belief with insulation of being decent people and obeying the rules, as if this will convince God to do as we expect and not allow anything bad to happen to us. Then a bomb falls on our cozy home and the walls are blown away, leaving us standing vulnerable, hurting, and cursing God for not keeping his end of the deal. We are left to put together the pieces. As John Claypool says, "We did not get our way." Is this a fair thing to do to God or ourselves? Experience tells us that we must die and that dying is a part of life.

Only God is God, and we do not understand God's mystery. Teilhard de Chardin explains the mystery by affirming that creation is incomplete and evolving. In *On Suffering*, he argues that the things in the world that kill us—disease, accidents, natural causes—are not divine, nor any way willed by God. They simply "represent that portion of incompleteness and disorder which mars a creation, that is still imperfectly unified. . . . God fights with us against them, and one day God will triumph."

Looking for Hope

The first time I remember really appreciating the two large hydrangea bushes in bloom on the edge of our patio was when a high school Spanish teacher in a work team said, "That is a glorious hydrangea."

"Yes, it is," I replied. It must have been in June, and the bushes were full of large, light blue, firm balls of petals. My heart was in a winter mood of deadness and hibernation rather than one of blossoming fullness.

Later, as winter came, the hydrangea bushes paralleled my emotions and turned brown. The leaves fell off, but the blooming petals stayed firm even in their brown state.

In my own state of winter, I found that there were firm securities that did not fail. These securities were no longer pretty, but they stayed together like the blooms on that hydrangea bush. During the year different images gave me security and hope for survival.

One image was that of Jonah. I imagined that I was thrown into the stormy sea and like Jonah, was carried along to safety by a large fish. In the back of my mind, I knew that the fish that carried me was God. God sent many people, memories, and wisdom, which together acted like Jonah's whale to carry me through. I smiled to myself as I thought I could tell those who helped us, "Thanks, you've been like a whale to me." Like Jonah's, my attitude following the storm was up to me. I had to decide how I would spend the rest of my life.

The brown hydrangea blooms kept a firm form throughout the winter months. I hoped that I, too, could remain firm in my marriage, firm in my faith, and firm in my remembrances of Hannah.

Kelly thought of ways to mark our remembrances of Hannah. At Christmas, she suggested decorating a special angel tree in Hannah's memory. She told me her idea right before she asked me to go to the van and unload the tree she had just purchased. We adorned the tree with angel ornaments and ornaments that Hannah had made. We had some ornaments that contained Hannah's picture. Kelly picked the brown hydrangea blooms and spray-painted them gold. Along with gold garland and tiny white lights, the hydrangea blooms provided a beautiful accent to Hannah's angel tree. Those golden hydrangea blooms also accented the green garland in our den.

We had an unusually mild winter that year in Piedmont. On one January day, I noticed that the large brown hydrangea bush had two small green sprigs emerging from a brown stalk. I stopped and noticed the absurdity of the light green shoots in the midst of winter. The budding tiny green leaves represented new life, hope, and a new beginning. I prayed that my broken and chilled heart might begin to notice green shoots of new life. I anxiously watched the green shoots on the bush. The premature shoots were blooming out of season and wilted after the first cold night.

It takes a great deal of patience to wait for new life to come. Nature teaches us the slow process of waiting until the right season for new growth and blooming. In *Zorba the Greek*, Nikos Kazantzakis writes about this process:

> I remembered one morning when I discovered a cocoon in the bark of a tree, just as a butterfly was making a hole in its case and preparing to come out. I waited a while, but it was too long appearing and I was impatient. I bent over it and breathed on it to warm it. I warmed it as quickly as I could and the miracle began to happen before my eyes, faster than life. The case opened, the butterfly started slowly crawling

out and I shall never forget my horror when I saw how its wings were folded back and crumpled; the wretched butterfly tried with its whole trembling body to unfold them. Bending over it, I tried to help it with my breath. In vain.

It needed to be hatched out patiently and the unfolding of the wings should be a gradual process in the sun: Now it was too late. My breath had forced the butterfly to appear, all crumpled, before its time. It struggled desperately and, a few seconds later, died in the palm of my hand.

That little body is, I do believe, the greatest weight I have on my conscience, for I realize today that it is a mortal sin to violate the great laws of nature. We should not hurry, we should not be impatient, but we should confidently obey the eternal rhythm.

I've never been good at waiting. I want to recover from the tragedy quickly. Counselors have told us that it will take years to fully recover—whatever "full recovery" is. Transformation is a slow process and takes patience. To pretend to be back to a new "normal" too soon sets us up to be hurt by the winter. One year seems like an eternity to quickaholics like me.

Healing is slow. The warm days of March brought a symphony of green shoots to the brown stems of the hydrangea bush. I began to break off and release the brown, dead balls that remained on the ends of the stalks. The March winds quickly swept these blooms away, making room for new life. All year long I had been looking for and grasping for signs of hope and new life. The green leaves continued to grow, and by the end of March, the bush was quite full of green, vibrant life. The blooms opened slowly. I had to wait several more months.

Marking the Time

On a beautiful morning in March, I was walking in the woods and praying. I prayed that God would help me know what I needed to do about several of my life struggles. I looked down, and there was a half-moon-shaped husk, which at one time had held a walnut. I was immediately drawn to the husk and leaned down and picked it up. As I looked at the smooth surface of the inner bowl, I thought about how within that shell a walnut was formed. The shell was not particularly rough compared to the meat of a walnut. What I was holding was the incubator, the cocoon for one nut. This external shell went to a great deal of trouble for one nut. I took the nut for granted, with no appreciation for the home that raised the nut. In order for a walnut to accomplish its purpose, the shell must crack open to let a new sprout emerge. For over an hour I carried that external shell, the womb of a nut, and contemplated the grace and pain of letting go.

In my life there has been much letting go. Yet in my own grief, I also try to keep Hannah alive by telling stories about her and laughing with her and discussing how she would have responded to certain things. Keeping her things as sacred relics helps me remember her life. I can keep these memories as I let go of my dreams for her life. I must let go of my hopes for her life. I must let go of her friends and the daily joys and challenges that her life brought. Eventually, I must let go of even the time-consuming memories in order to get on with my life. I must move on and not dwell on her life. This is the most painful part of grief—letting go and moving on. Yet if we are to live, we must let go of things we love and take up new things.

Letting go involves little deaths and prepares us for facing our own death. Over a lifetime, we have many opportunities to face small deaths and embrace pain, only to experience rebirth. How do we learn that our bodies are not our own? In 1 Corinthians 6:12-20, we are reminded that we are creatures created by God. At Hannah's baptism, Kelly and I handed her over to the pastor. We acknowledged that she was in God's hands, and we gave her to God and the church.

It was as though we acknowledged that she was not ours but God's.

Baptism is a way we practice and remind ourselves to give our children to God. If I had taken her baptism more seriously or thought about it more deeply perhaps I could have dealt better with her death. Those who criticize the church as being uninteresting and having no bite or challenge today are simply not listening to the radical nature of this baptismal challenge of giving ourselves and our children to God. When I think I have truly given myself or my children to God, then I quickly must take back myself and my children, for I really want to keep control of my life, and keep my children close by. This is just one of the many contradictions of my life.

When we are close to death, death becomes a teacher that helps us live. The story of our family's tragedy was enough to move strangers to want to let go and die to self and experience a rebirth. We received many letters from people who had been moved by the story and had decided to do something positive in response. One person had carried around a resentment toward another person for twenty years and after the tornado decided it was time to contact that person and try to work things out. She needed to let go of that resentment before she could move on. The only way she could let go was to confront her problem.

The little husk I found in the forest, which allowed the nut inside it to leave, was forever changed by that walnut. When the walnut left, the husk was no longer the same. I, too, must let go of who I thought I was before the tornado. I am now a different person.

As Hannah embraced the great mystery of death, I too experienced a death to self, and a rebirth. Albert Camus knew that embracing death is an important factor in discovering meaning in our lives. Death forces us to work to make our remaining minutes precious and sacred and worthwhile. Death gives us the courage to sort out our priorities regarding how to use our remaining time on earth. As I contemplated leaving my job and beginning a new, unknown journey, I had a strange and humorous thought: "The worst that could happen to me is death, and that wouldn't be so bad. So what is there to lose?" When we embrace death, it becomes a friend. If we are wise, death can give us the courage to avoid obsessions of hoarding, having, conquering, and separating, and give us the energy to spend time and energy on important, positive aspects of living.

This is what Odysseus learned in Homer's *Iliad* and *Odyssey*. In the course of his many heroic adventures, Odysseus sailed to Hades, where he saw the great Greek heroes of the past. In death they were nothing and wanted only news from the world. Through facing his future death, Odysseus realized that what would endure beyond his life would be his relationships with his wife and son, and not his exploits and adventures. His lasting legacy would be those he influenced at home.

How do we let go and embrace pain? In our culture we have natural rituals that "mark the time" and give the hurting community an opportunity to grieve. In the United States common rituals include a visitation time at the funeral home, which allows friends and family to see the body of the deceased. This also allows people to show that they care for the grieving family with expressions of flowers and hugs. Funeral services and memorial services are also rituals that help us embrace the pain and have a sense of closure. But often these rituals happen too soon after the death for the family, and more rituals are needed to help families embrace their pain, let go, and heal.

Beginning just after I learned of Hannah's death, I wrote out my feelings and perceptions of what was happening in journals. Writing these journals took a great deal of time, but it was my way of embracing the pain a little at a time so that healing could occur. Reflecting upon the images and stories that fill this writing brings healing and perhaps even gives the experience meaning for me. "Any sorrow can be borne if a story can be told about it," said Isak Dinesen. So we can tell the stories and create ways of telling the story little by little.

We need to express our feelings in some way. One of the most meaningful ways of expressing ourselves is to create something. Expressing ourselves through art and poetry is healing for the soul. Our souls need to be unveiled through the arts. We lash out at one another, partly because our inner selves need to release their energy. This released energy can be harnessed in creative ways.

One friend paints with watercolors. After the tornado, she began to paint and allow her innermost images and feelings to emerge. When she finished she had painted a tornado, and Hannah ascending from the church and tornado with a palm branch in her hand. This was a wonderful, healing way for this artist to pray and be with us. She reluctantly decided to send us the painting, with hopes that it would help and not hurt us. We loved it and found it healing and touching.

Several people from our support group decided to purchase trunks to hold the special belongings of those who died. Kelly said that the store had either black or blue, so of course we got blue. Some other families also got blue trunks. In our trunk are drawings and paintings by Hannah, as well as some favorite toys and books. Over the years the trunk will be filled with treasures that remind us of Hannah's precious life.

Just eight weeks after Hannah's death, I attended a friendly church where my friend was the pastor. I did not realize that it was Memorial Day, and as a church, they would be allowing people to share sacred memories of loved ones who had died. My friend asked the congregation to informally turn to someone around them and share a remembrance. Tears were streaming down my face, and I could only nod. Finally, I said it was just too close for me to talk about. Following this sharing time, a hymn was sung and as I read the words the congregation sang, I began to weep. I wept throughout the rest of the service. At the time, I didn't welcome the pain and thought that if I had known what they were doing, I would not have gone to that church. But in retrospect, I realize those were healing tears and needed to flow. I remember it as one of the best opportunities I had to grieve silently in the midst of a crowd of strangers who cared and who were not afraid to allow me to cry as they sang the words I could not sing.

Kelly uses creative energy to mark the time. Throughout this year she has invited me to make an ordinary moment and space sacred through a ritual of words and tears. In a way these ritualistic practices are like offering a blessing and prayer for the deceased. It can be as simple as lighting a candle with a prayer for the person's peace. Often as we perform these simple rituals, we feel as if we are offering Hannah our blessing. The ritual may be writing a letter, or starting a scrapbook with important memories and pictures of our time together.

One of Kelly's projects has been to create a wonderful scrapbook with pages that tell of the different parts of Hannah's life. One page has pictures of Hannah with animals. One is dedicated to Hannah's baptism. Other pages include pictures of Hannah and her dolls, with her cousins, with her sister, at holidays. Kelly has spent hours going through old pictures and developing this scrapbook. She calls it her time to grieve. It is not easy, but embracing the pain allows our souls time to heal.

Hannah's birthday was July 21. I left work early, and Kelly and I went back to the backyard where Hannah had played for three years. (We moved to that house when she was ten months old.) We had a balloon bouquet, and both of us climbed up upon a three-foot stump, which before the tornado had held the swing and rope that Hannah had loved. We stood on the stump and one at a time gave a short blessing for something we loved about Hannah. With each blessing, we would release a balloon and watch it ascend into the mystery—a gift to her. We thought it appropriate to be standing on a stump, because Hannah always wanted to climb on top of something wherever she was. It was a touching tribute shared only by us. It was painful, yet healing.

"I miss the passion you had to climb and climb."

And we released a blue balloon.

"I miss you telling me that you love me. And I miss telling you I love you."

We released a yellow balloon.

"I miss your noise and the way you would never allow me to sit quietly and do anything."

We laughed, and a pink balloon ascended.

"I miss the way you would make up silly rhyming word games, and we would laugh together."

We released a green balloon.

"I miss the delight and joy you brought us."

An orange balloon flies upward.

I admit that I felt silly standing on a stump with a bunch of balloons on a hot afternoon, but frankly, no one even noticed or cared. One of my professors used to tell us that we wasted far too much energy worrying about what people thought of us. If we really knew how little people did pay attention to what we did, we would be very depressed.

It is a sacred moment when as a pastor I lift up the bread and break it in the Eucharistic service. The eyes of the congregation watch me as I lift up the cup and say the words they must have heard hundreds of times, "The body of Christ broken for you. The blood of Christ shed for you." The community of faith gives these acts respect and a holiness. As I have pictured how I lift up a sacred memory or think about Hannah's life, I imagine that I am holding it up as I hold up the sacred elements. I give them to God, to Hannah, to the angels and archangels, and they join with me in sharing this sacred time, just as in Eucharist. Each time I offer my own brokenness and pain, I know that God is no stranger to grief and suffering. Healing has come to me when I have been able to lift up a memory or a hurt. When I begin to offer the pains up, then through naming it, I can accept it, and a little bit of the pain is taken from me.

Thomas Moore, in *Care of the Soul*, tells us that one part of caring for our souls or spiritual lives is to create the holy or sacred in our ordinary lives. I believe that the more we practice treating the works of God's creation as sacred, the better we will become at treating ourselves as sacred, and treating those around us as sacred. Each of us has sacred things in our home—things we decide are more precious than others. If we had a china cabinet, we would use it to display a glass bowl that was a wedding gift to Kelly's grandmother. That bowl is not worth much in the world of glass bowls—it might go for a dollar in a yard sale—but to us it is sacred because of whose bowl it was and the emotions and hopes that it represented to Kelly.

It is an intentional act to call something special. We have a doll that was Hannah's "very nice" doll. Hannah dressed it in its prettiest Easter dress to go to a wedding the day before she died. Sarah wants to play with that doll, but we keep it in the special blue trunk. Sarah knows it is very special, and does play with it sometimes. Even at three years old, Sarah knows to treat this special doll with reverence.

In October 1994, Goshen United Methodist Church had a memorial service for all those who died in the storm. It was roughly six months after the tornado. One of the most surprising things that helped each family was writing a short statement about the person who died for the memorial booklet. It was not an easy thing to do, but it proved quite healing. For another ritual, a long altar table was placed at the front of the sanctuary. Each family brought something that represented the deceased person and placed it on the altar. Among the items adorning the altar were pictures, dolls, children's paintings, a baseball hat, a sculpture of an extended hand, a baby toy, a military medal of honor, and a nurse's cap. Kelly held up well in organizing and planning the service. Our family and dear friends from Maryland and Virginia came

to be with us. Kelly read the names aloud, slowly and rever-
ently. Returning to her seat, she caught a glimpse of the rare
sight of her father's face clenched with sorrow. She broke
down and cried as the hymn began. It was not until this point,
over six months later, that our entire grief could even be
grasped. This marked a watershed in our lives. One by one
the twenty who died were honored by all who attended. It
was one more way of marking time and offering a blessing.
For those of us who were grieving, it was an opportunity to
cry together. I had not cried at Hannah's funeral, but I did
not stop crying at the memorial service. The tears were
healing, and would not have occurred had we not intentionally marked the time and made sacred the ordinary. This
service gave me a ritual to embrace the pain and to let go a
little more.

We honor people in numerous ways. It is important not to
forget those who have shaped our lives, and so I would
suggest that a way to remember is to offer acts of remembrance: for example, undertaking a memorial project, purchasing gifts for someone else for your loved one's birthday,
or giving to a charity in your loved one's memory. It is good
for the soul to remember, and it is good for the soul to give
beyond ourselves.

On March 27, 1995, the first anniversary of the tornado,
Kelly and I simply sat on the couch in our den and placed a
candle on the coffee table. We lit the candle. Breaking the
silence, we both reflected upon our lives and how we had
changed in the past year. Lighting a candle is a simple act,
but verbalizing the deep things in your life is never a simple
or easy thing to do. This ritual did not take a long time, but
it had more power than I could have anticipated. Taking time
to delight in and cherish our children is perhaps the most
important task of parents. Since I cannot delight in Hannah's
new life, I must delight in my memories. But I am careful not
to diminish the delight I continue to have in Sarah's life as
she continues to grow, dance, climb, and hope.

On Easter Sunday, 1995, we dedicated "Hannah's Playground" at Camp Sumatanga, our United Methodist Camp in northern Alabama. It was built from donations from around the world. We were touched that over one thousand families had made contributions. This experience was another way of marking the time, and feeling the love and care that was expressed by those who donated to the fund. As I wrote the litany for the dedication of the playground, I cried with sadness and with joy:

Leader: Ever living God, this resurrection day revives in us memories of Hannah Kathryn Clem. What happiness we shared when she danced and sang in our lives. What joy and anxiety she brought to us as she climbed to the highest points of playgrounds. Her love for us, and for life, touched us, and stirred our love for one another and for life. We give thanks for her life, and our sacred memories. Hannah walks with us still.

People: Hannah's memory is a blessing forever. Her spirit lives on in this place. Her soul is bound up in ours forever.

Leader: The mystery of death is not just an ending, but a beginning. After the storm a rainbow appears. We celebrate that grains of a thousand seeds have joined together to make this playground rise as communion bread, giving joy and nourishment to all who play and watch here.

People: Like the rainbow, the playground is a sign of love and hope.

Leader: As Hannah was fresh from God, she refreshed our hearts with laughter. Fresh from God, she rekindled our imaginations to play. Fresh from God, she reminded us of the wonder and delight in creation. Fresh from God, she revealed a security where she could trust. Fresh from God, she loved to sing.

People: Her songs live on through the laughter and joy heard on this site.

Leader: When the disciples were trying to keep the children from touching the master, Jesus said, "Let the little children come to me; do not stop them; for it is to such as these that the kingdom of God belongs. Truly I tell you, whoever does not receive the kingdom of God as a little child will never enter it."

People: "And He took them up in his arms, laid his hands on them, and blessed them" (Mark 10:14-16).

Leader: When the disciples asked Jesus, " 'Who is the greatest in the kingdom of heaven?' [Jesus] called a child . . . and said ' . . . Whoever becomes humble like this child is the greatest in the kingdom of heaven. Whoever welcomes one such child in my name welcomes me' " (Matthew 18:1-5).

People: Let the children come!
Leader: All followers of Christ are children of God.
People: Let the children come!
Leader: Let us pray:

Eternal God, bless this playground.
    Let your love rest upon it and your promised presence
    be manifested in it through joy, laughter and praise.
    We commit into your care, all who pray here, and play here,
    that they will grow in their love for you and their love for all of creation.
    On this resurrection day, we dedicate this playground to your enjoyment and service.
    In the name of the Father, and of the Son, and of the Holy Spirit.

People: Amen! Let the children come!

Sarah cut the ribbon to the playground. At three, she does not remember it, but she will remember it as we tell the story of the playground and her sister. About four hundred people attended the dedication, many of whom were children. We had an Easter egg hunt, pony rides, and a visit from the Easter Bunny. The children had a great time, and we had a sacred moment to mark the rebirth following death.

It has been through embracing the pain in small, simple ways that Kelly and I have begun to let go and heal. The liturgies of the church's season include anticipation, self-searching, joy, celebration, suffering, self-denial, death, resurrection, and moving beyond ourselves into service. Many of these themes we would try to avoid; yet the church asks us to confront such matters, which, although they are painful, prepare us to live, and live meaningfully.

The Path of Growth and Maturity

The creation story in Genesis says that God created human beings in God's own image. Milton and many others have struggled with whether this image is good or bad. We want to say that God is only good—but our sight is limited. The psalmist says, "You have made [human beings] a little lower than God, and crowned them with glory and honor" (Psalm 8:5). Not only are we images of God, but we are also royal and holy. Both Exodus 19:6 and the baptismal hymn recorded in 1 Peter 2:9-10 speak of a chosen people, a royal priesthood. Not only are we "images of God," royal and holy, but we are also "words" that God spoke when God spoke creation into being (Ephesians 1:4). Perhaps it was these scriptures that caused Teilhard de Chardin to ask, Are we human beings with a spiritual experience, or spiritual beings with a human experience?

Simply polishing an idolized self-esteem is not helpful. The reality is that I am an incomplete creation and not God. If I am so wonderful, why do I make so many mistakes? After the tornado, I did things I could never imagine doing. I watched Kelly and others who performed miraculous, compassionate acts of kindness and love. There was no doubt that, deep down inside, people are capable of being royal and holy. Our holiness has to do with all the habits the church cultivates in us and our created goodness—every aspect of our life in communion with God and one another. But our holiness is also called for, even when we doubt any holiness exists within us.

Like Jonah, we may not realize our holiness and abilities until we are cast into the deep, into the heart of the sea. It is then that our spark of the image of God can be drawn closer to the likeness of God. Irenaeus, in the second century, said that the image of God is at our deepest level and we can never lose it. The likeness of God is that which we must strive to grow into. The faith community calls each of us to live this life of holiness.

The New Testament writers teach that this maturity does not occur at once, but is a process. It occurs through a series of tests and movements from darkness to light. The essence of our sacred worth is within us all along. Trials and difficult experiences have the potential to bring us closer to God.

This is exactly what Christian baptism is all about. We enter into the waters of rebirth and arise a new person. Baptism symbolically allows a person to be taken under the cleansing waters of death and rise up as a new person. The early church often built baptismal fonts in the shape of tombs to remind Christians that we are called to die to self.

We find ourselves in an unfamiliar situation. We are afraid, and the way looks dark. Individually we are challenged to stretch our wings and find within us resources of wisdom and courage to respond. It is up to us to figure out how best to allow God's light to illuminate the darkness with new possibilities. When we emerge, the lessons we have learned can be great. The light gives us a new perspective.

All of us are on the hero's journey of facing and overcoming trials and hardships. The good news from our journey through darkness is that there is a power when we trust our own abilities and God's grace to lead us through the labyrinth.

We must enter the depths of our souls and risk losing control before we can emerge transformed. Jonah finds himself going into the depths of darkness in the belly of a whale and coming forth transformed. We enter the darkness to die to living only for ourselves. We go to the depths to be remolded in God's likeness. In the dark, we face the mystery of who we are and who God is calling us to be. Jesus is constantly inviting us to go deeper into ourselves. While in the depth and darkness of the cave, the tomb, the womb, we create a sacred space for the songs within us to come forth. There are within us more songs, thoughts, feelings, and heroic deeds than we ever imagine.

It is in the belly of the fish, the cave, the tomb, that we are able to listen for God's questions and God's knocking. In the silence and darkness we are awakened to new emotions and respect for others and ourselves. In the belly of the cave we learn to rely upon God's grace. Relating to Jonah made the lines from Carl Sandburg's poem "Losers" powerful.

> If I should pass the tomb of Jonah,
> I think I would stop there and sit for a while
> Because I was swallowed one time deep in the dark
> and came out alive after all.

The question is always before me: Have I emerged from the belly? If I analyze my patience, the answer would be no. Perhaps the proper attitude is thankfulness that I have received and continue to receive gifts of grace.

The hardest step for me is to admit that I have far to go toward maturity. It's hard to be open to God's gifts of grace when I am so busy trying to work it out for myself. When a friend said to me, "You seem like you have matured lately," I wasn't sure I wanted to admit that I was not yet mature at my age. But my heart knew my immaturity. My heart had been working hard to speak the truth without avoiding and dancing around pain. My heart said thank you to my friend for having the courage to speak directly to me about how he saw me growing. Following the conversation, I listened to the internal debate that followed. A part of me regretted that I had allowed my immaturity to show. It seemed to be the heart, but it could have been simply God's grace, that answered lovingly, "But you can only be what you are at any given time. Even in heaven, there will be new paths of growth. Don't torture yourself; celebrate the fact that you are not stagnant but on the journey."

Surviving, but Not Without Tensions

For many months following the tornado, I found music intolerable. Then I came to the place when I listened to slow, somber music. I longed to hear a nice, simple Bach chorale. At the end of the day, when Kelly and I had our quiet time together, several times I would start to play some music, and she would say, "No, I just can't take any sounds or movement." We were at different places in our grief. By Christmas, we could both listen to music together if it was quiet, soothing music. I couldn't imagine listening to a fast, happy Mozart piece, which I had loved prior to the tornado. By the time the one-year anniversary passed, Kelly and I could both tolerate different kinds of music. What voice was within us that either enjoyed, craved, or couldn't tolerate music? Music finds a way into our depths that is not rational or conscious. Our safe passage through the musical desert and arrival in one piece on the other side was a good sign.

After the one-year anniversary passed, Kelly looked at me with a grin and said, "We survived!" Surviving was amazing. A one-year anniversary of Hannah's death somehow gave us confidence and a sense of accomplishment.

John Claypool states that in the adult years we have three main tasks: developing our identity, developing our relationships, and developing our vocations. In his book *Stages,* Claypool points out that it is overwhelming to have to work on all three issues at once. Many people become successful in one area such as vocation, and inadequate in their relationships with others (spouse, children, friends) and their own identity. To illustrate, he cites King David in the Bible as one who was developed in his vocation, but a failure in the other two developmental issues of his adult life.

Grief throws one into the difficult work of dealing with all three of these frontiers at once. It is a gift of grace if at least one of these life issues is stable and flexible enough to allow work on the other two. Working on all three at once can be time-consuming and paralyzing.

If you hit a middle C on the piano, you will hear the primary note of C. But you will also hear overtones of other notes, which give depth and layers that support the sound. "We Survived!" is a middle C we were proud to celebrate, but Kelly and I heard layers of other notes as well. If we pretended that some dissonant notes did not make up the overtone chord, we would be dishonest. The wonderful thing about dissonance in music and in life is that there is hope that chords and our lives can be transformed into a major chord of triumph. The painful part of transforming the dissonant note into the major chord involves befriending it enough so that it is absorbed into the new chord. The painful emotions such as anger and despair are to be felt and not overcome. When we try to separate ourselves from the negative emotions, they gain power and threaten our balance. Without dissonant notes, the music of our lives would be much less real and meaningful.

It was the "whys" that helped us face those dissonant notes and absorb them into the major chords again. Kelly and I had many reasons to live. To be honest, one thing that surprised me is how little importance I placed on living as an example for others, or on surviving for the sake of the church. However, Kelly and I did think about those things quite often. The main challenge Kelly and I faced was creating a stable home for Sarah. Our parental roles caused our sense of responsibility and authority to continue functioning.

The Struggle with Marriage

Many told us that they hoped that this tragedy would draw Kelly and me closer together in our marriage. But grief is a private affair. Grief causes people to disappear within themselves. I'm not sure it is possible to share your grief with another, for it is hard enough to understand your own grief yourself. If someone had the courage to share his or her feelings and thoughts, it would be a rare person who could absorb the burden. A spouse whose heart is already full of grief simply doesn't have the energy to reach out and absorb the grief of the other spouse.

It is easier to share the escapes from grief than it is to share the pain of grief. Redecorating, a night out, away from the responsibilities of home life, and even vacations are wonderful escapes that unite a grieving couple. We enjoyed them all. But even on our escapes, my mind would wander and I would find myself isolating myself and withdrawing. It was as if an unconscious mistress was demanding my attention. Daydreaming is an important part of grief work. Fortunately, I had an understanding wife who, though she was irritated by my side trips, would laugh with me and bring me back by singing the *Twilight Zone* theme song—her way of asking, "Anybody home?"

I shared the hope that this tragedy would bring Kelly and me together, but I also knew that when we left the cemetery, our marriage was automatically on thin ice. The reality is that initially a family is brought closer by the horror of grief, but after leaving the cemetery, any dysfunctions that previously existed in the family are amplified. If there are notes that are out of tune before the death, they will not get tuned up because of the death. The notes are simply played louder and become more annoying.

A basic problem that Kelly and I discovered is that we grieve differently and on different schedules. After several months of tension, we realized that we had to do a better job of communicating and sharing what was happening in our lives. At night, after Sarah went to bed, Kelly was often still working, and I was depressed and simply went to bed early. We decided to purchase a hot tub, and we made a standing date with each other in the tub at ten o'clock each night for unwinding and conversation. I have said that the hot tub "saved our marriage." Kelly thought that this statement was too strong, and she was right. But finding time we could spend together was essential in keeping our relationship alive. We said it to ourselves and to one another: "Let's just keep communicating, and we will work through this tragedy."

We did not pretend that we could fill each other's needs. Sharing and absorbing each other's pain simply wasn't possible. We both needed friends and community outside of each other who could be strong enough to absorb the pain of our grief. Only a special person can travel into the depths of pain with another. Without that support system, I do not know how anyone could survive loss.

Psychiatrist M. Scott Peck, in *The Road Less Traveled*, defined love as "the will to extend one's self for the purpose of nurturing one's own or another's spiritual growth." In a marriage, we must create a sacred space for our own growth. We must learn to play our own music before we can play confidently in the duet of marriage. The mystery of love is that one can only be fulfilled in giving to the other. The temptation is to play a duet when neither has developed his or her own songs. When we have not developed our own music to bring to the marriage, then our relationship is not based on giving but on receiving. "Since I don't love me and don't have a song, I need to use you to love me and give me a song."

There were many days when work for me was completely draining, for I needed time alone to think, ponder, and grieve. Kelly, by contrast, felt a great sense of urgency in throwing herself into her work as pastor. Kelly and I understood that each of us was dealing with Hannah's death in our own way and in our own time. She gave me space to be silent, and waited for me to speak. We trusted that as we emerged from the depths of grief, we would be different people, but we would be different people who were still married.

In typical male fashion, I had trouble verbalizing my feelings and expressing what I was thinking. Often, I would sit listening to Kelly's many words, and sometimes she would sit patiently waiting for me to express my thoughts. Then there would be a long silence, and I would simply laugh. During the silence, I would be responding and thinking about what Kelly had said, but silently. I would laugh because I realized I just couldn't find the right words to express my thoughts. I wanted Kelly to read my mind. I laughed a lot about how I expected Kelly to read my mind, so I would not have to speak. In *Naming the Silences,* Stanley Hauerwas expresses this tension well:

> Tolstoy observed that all happy marriages are similar, but all unhappy marriages are different. There seems something right about this observation, though it is by no means easy to say why. I suspect the difference between happiness and suffering is that the latter creates a silence which is not easily shared. No two sufferings are the same: my suffering, for example, occurs in the

context of my personal history and thus is peculiarly mine. Few of us have the gift to tell the story of our suffering in a manner that enables us to share it with others. The gift as well as the burden of the artist is to be able to tell the story so that others may have some idea of what his or her suffering is like.

In *Letters to a Young Poet,* Rainer Maria Rilke writes, "For one human being to love another is perhaps the most difficult task of all, the epitome, the ultimate test. It is that striving for which all other striving is merely preparation."

Perhaps under the best of circumstances, the small things are what annoy us in a marriage. But when you are in grief, a small jab either feels as if it came from a professional boxer, or it isn't even noticed. Fortunately, Kelly and I came to an understanding that our reactions or overreactions to the small, annoying things we did were simply not very important. If we were avoiding a larger issue beneath the little irritations, there would be time to deal with it when we were stronger. At the time, we needed each other too much to fight over silly things. Yet perhaps it is inevitable in human nature to wound those you love and need the most. I read once that there is always a shadow side of light. Even faith, hope, and love have their shadows, which can ultimately lead to betrayal.

When something is bothering me, I need simply to state it. Whether I can find the courage and the appropriate way to express it is another matter. However, once I get it out, it has lost its power over me, and I can go on with the relationship. I am not saying that every sour note in our music needs to be expressed to our spouse. Attacking and wounding just to make ourselves feel better is not helpful in a relationship. There is wisdom in knowing when to speak and when to keep silent and find other ways to creatively express your feelings. There are a variety of ways to release the energy behind the festering hurts and disappointments that drive a wedge in a relationship.

We Are All Connected

On Palm Sunday, 1995, about four hundred people gathered in downtown Piedmont for a Palm Sunday processional. It was a time to remember and support one another. There is something powerful about walking together. There is a solidarity that comes from walks. Many great walks have changed history: Gandhi's salt march in 1930, and the Civil Rights' demonstrators' walk from Selma to Montgomery in 1965. After Jesus' death, the disciples were walking down the road, and a stranger walked with them. Only later did they recognize that it was Jesus who was walking with them. Throughout the past year, Kelly and I have felt that we were never walking alone. God has been walking beside us through strangers and friends, and in ways in which he was unrecognizable. God is still walking in this garden we call earth. How do we know God is walking with us? There is no way to prove it, other than by the love of friends, strangers, and a feeling.

As I walked, my heart was both sad and grateful. It had been a tough year. As Peter, Paul, and Mary sing, "It's no easy walk to freedom," and it had not been an easy walk through the past year. The road had been stony and rough. At times I had been stuck in a ditch on the side of the road. Sometimes, I had to stop. But throughout the walk, we felt the amazing presence of others walking with us. Many times I felt isolated, for grief pursues a lonely path. But friends kept coming to walk with me. On this Palm Sunday walk, I was grateful for all those who walked with us, those who said prayers, those who sent gifts and cards, those who visited and worked in the community building houses or cutting trees, those who played with our children. We have walked on a road of God's grace all year long.

The walk through life is not a solitary journey, but a journey enriched by the footprints of those who walked before us, the footprints of those who walk beside us, and the footprints of the One who sometimes carries us on our journey into the great mystery of death. Throughout this walk, God has been walking along in the garden called Earth saying, "Where are you?"

Life As a Pond

As I think of God walking in the garden asking, "Where are you?" I have come to think of my life as a pond. Many questions come to mind as I contemplate my life as a pond. The tornado has certainly made a big impact. However, the pond, my life, was here before the tornado, and it is still here. I hope I continue to be fed from the waters of God. My life, like the waters in a pond, is constantly changing and stirring. Each life event is like a pebble that comes into the pond and causes ripples. The splash may be remembered as a small or large circle, although to look at us, one would rarely guess that the pebble caused waves; for the waves have dissipated. On the surface, there is visible action, but beneath the water's surface there are many unknown layers of feelings and memories.

If the pond is alive, the water must flow in and out. If the pond is dying, the water becomes stagnant and smells. Underneath, there are secret springs of water that feed our ponds. God's grace sometimes comes to us from the depths, and sometimes from the rain above. God's grace and nudging comes to us like a pebble that is thrown into the water and causes gentle and quiet ripples to expand across the face of the water. God's grace may sometimes come as a huge splash, which causes waves to disrupt the water's surface. But often God's grace feeds us from beneath the surface in unknown ways and brings us knowledge and grace while its source remains a mystery. I have sat at water's edge and watched the surface of the water, and occasionally an air bubble rises to the surface. Where did that bubble come from? Was there a turtle down there? Often we do not understand the bubbles that rise from the depths of our being.

My life is like a pond. Each time I have an "aha moment" and learn something new, it is like a pebble has come into my water and caused ripples to expand across the surface. In our pond, one event or circle of our individual lives sends ripples to all parts of our lives, even if very slightly.

The waters of one pond affect the water of another. Our waters cannot be separated from the waters of another. The deeper we move into God's grace, the deeper we move into unknown mysteries of ourselves, and the connections of the world. When the deep streams beneath the surface connect, they create a pool, and it is from this pool that our wells draw.

How do we grow? Do we grow deeper, wider, or do we have a balanced ecosystem? Do we have clear water? What happens if our ponds grow into lakes? How do we know our limits and boundaries? Do my waters expand as they flow outward into the world? If we are not careful in letting our water out we become shallow, and we miss out on some of those underground streams to feed us in the dry months.

There are dangers, such as toxic waste and chemicals, that threaten the life of my pond. There is the possibility that our boundaries slip too low and our waters are mixed with another's waters; we live in a flood and lose all sense of who we are. We are codependent, and our identity is fused with the identity of another.

From my childhood I remember the yearly task of cleaning out a spring that fed a little pond near my grandparents' home. Each year, we had to clean out the spring to assure that the spring water would be pure and have a clear path. Writing this book has been like cleaning out the spring. I have looked at many things and gotten many thoughts out of my system. It was a task of passion and healing. Often we do not know what we feel or think until we state it out loud or write it down. The question remains for me: What still needs cleaning out in order to enhance the clarity and balance of my pond?

The questions are endless as we explore the question God asks of us, "Where are you?" Muddy waters keep us from seeing clearly, and perhaps we need friends and pastors to help us find clarity. Perhaps it is in the stories of others that we find our own feelings and thoughts. This book has been an attempt to share my story with the hopes that the reader will be able to lean over the water's edge and see his or her own reflection, or the reflection of others.

The wonderful thing about life is that cleansing waters come, and we are able to breathe new life and start over. As the reader will note, the pond I have explored in this book has changed significantly as I have moved through the year. Healing waters of love and grace have softened the deep pain of grief. I hope I will continue to clean out the springs and look at the waters of my life and the waters of other ponds. Caring for our ponds is no small task, for the waters we care for are not ours alone. These precious waters are the ponds of the future.

Life Is Deeper and Richer

I'm not sure when I began to notice that I was living life at a deeper and richer level than before the tornado. I immediately knew that my perspective on normal life activities had changed, but living life at a richer level is a mystery. It is hard for me to understand, and more difficult to explain. I may express it by an exaggerated metaphor: Before the tornado I saw the world in only a few colors. After the tornado, in the healing process, I began to see many brilliant, rich colors. I don't mean to say that before the tornado, I was blind to colors, tastes, smells, and sound, but now I notice and appreciate them at a deeper level. I do not take the beauty of ordinary experiences for granted, as I did before. There are so many sights and sounds to hear and see if we simply listen and look. There are dozens of sounds coming from an "empty" field. How many different wildflowers are growing in a ditch near your home? Sarah is playing with the dog and suddenly she stands frozen in wonder. "Did you know that there are flowers in the grass?" She picks a handful of them, drops them in front of Kelly, and says, "These flowers remind me of heaven." Then she resumes her wrestle with the dog. Have you seen the graceful way some flowers open and close daily? I love to stand in the damp stillness of dawn and watch the way the sun rises and creates a strange and hopeful half light. I attempt to savor and appreciate the gifts the senses bring me. Profound insights and grace can come through the ordinary path of life.

This change has come through a process change in my value system. I have realized that living in the present is just as important as living for the future. I have realized that spending time with family and friends is of more value than working seventy-hour weeks, trying to make a name for myself. The ironic thing is that I talked about having these values before the tornado, but now I seem to be freer to live them with greater confidence than before. I knew the importance of love, family, and appreciating the present before, but living through the tragedy branded the truth into my heart and mind.

I pause and savor the tastes of food, and I delight in a good meal. I appreciate the sense of taste like never before. This did not develop right after the tornado, but over the period of the year. After the tornado, I was numb to taste. For months, nothing seemed to taste good. Then over time, I began to taste food and think: "I don't think this food has ever tasted so good." Kelly and I appreciate gourmet meals with special sauces and delightful tastes. A friend cooked mock turtle soup for lunch, and the memory of that delicious soup made me happy for a week. I enjoy more celebrations using fine china and cooking special meals. Before the tornado, food was sustenance and meals were times to enjoy our family. But now, I have realized that in simple meals, we can nourish not only the body but the soul. Meals are not an interruption from a busy day in which accomplishing goals is the priority. Meals can be opportunities to savor the joy of the moment. It is a gift of grace that allows me to enjoy the present without rushing out to make something happen in the future. It is also a practice of being attentive to the joys of life in the present. Enjoying a good meal is a way to enjoy God. And when you take time to enjoy a meal, you can take time to notice the ways God is moving and calling us in our lives.

Kelly and I both enjoy pleasant smells in the house. Why would you want to keep good smells in the house? It helps me live life on a deeper level and it nourishes my soul. I baked brownies last week, not because I wanted brownies, but because my soul needed the nourishment of the smell of brownies. Kelly has begun baking bread regularly. The smells give us life and good memories. The senses are windows into memory and soul. Leonard Sweet told us that he enjoys using a soap with a pine fragrance in his shower because it reminds him daily of the good memories of his childhood in the mountains.

When I walk through the woods, I notice more smells and see the tiny white, yellow, and purple flowers. I noticed them before the tornado, but I experience them differently now.

The arts have always been an interest to me, but grief has made me less tolerant of some art, and deeply moved by other. Hearing Stravinsky's Concertino performed by the Vermeer string quartet in Chicago left me breathless. The intensity of the music seemed to echo my own inner strings. There was a surprising resonance, and I turned to Kelly and said "That was my life!"

It is a rare occasion when I hear words and sentences put together eloquently. One day I was channel-surfing on the

TV and came across a tribute by Bill Moyers to Charles Kuralt. I have always admired both these men. In listening to Moyers's eloquent tribute, I was moved to tears. His superior use of language inspired me to work harder at the way I shaped images and sentences.

I don't know how to describe this change other than as an attempt to live at a deeper level of life. This is a gift of grief. Living at a deeper level for me means that I am more attentive to the calling of my soul. I acknowledge now that the yearning of my soul may be to give me insight, wisdom, and guidance.

I view this new way of seeing as a gift of grace. It teaches me that where one thing ends, something new begins. It is like the circle of grace itself. The circle continues in a new way. With every ending is a beginning.

WORKS CITED

Angelou, Maya. *I Know Why the Caged Bird Sings*. New York: Random House, 1970.

Becker, Ernest. *The Denial of Death*. New York: Free Press, 1973.

Buechner, Frederick. *Whistling in the Dark: A Doubter's Dictionary*. New York: HarperCollins, 1993.

Burns, Olive Ann. *Cold Sassy Tree*. New York: Ticknor and Fields, 1984.

Coles, Robert. *The Spiritual Life of Children*. Boston: Houghton Mifflin, 1990.

Cone, James H. *The Spirituals and the Blues*. Maryknoll, N.Y.: Orbis Books, 1991.

Hauerwas, Stanley. *Naming the Silences: God, Medicine, and the Problem of Suffering*. Grand Rapids, Mich.: Eerdmans, 1990.

Kazantzakis, Nikos. *Zorba the Greek*. New York: Touchtone, 1971.

Marty, Martin E. *A Cry of Absence: Reflections for the Winter of the Heart*. San Francisco: HarperSanFrancisco, 1992.

Merton, Thomas. *New Seeds of Contemplation*. New York: New Directions, 1961.

Moltmann, Jürgen. *The Crucified God: The Cross of Christ As the Foundation and Criticism of Christianity*. Minneapolis: Augsburg Fortress Press, 1993.

Moody, Raymond. *Reunions: Visionary Encounters with Departed Loved Ones*. New York: Random House, 1993.

Moore, Thomas. *Care of the Soul: A Guide for Cultivating Depth and Sacredness in Everyday Life*. New York: HarperCollins, 1992.

Naylor, Thomas, William Willimon, and Magdalena Naylor. *The Search for Meaning*. Nashville: Abingdon Press, 1994.

Palmer, Parker. *The Active Life: Wisdom for Work, Creativity, and Caring*. San Francisco: HarperSanFrancisco, 1991.

Peck, M. Scott. *The Road Less Traveled: A New Psychology of Love, Traditional Values and Spiritual Growth*. New York: Simon & Schuster, 1978.

Rilke, Rainer Maria. *Letters to a Young Poet*. Trans. M. D. Norton. New York: W. W. Norton, 1993.

Stafford, William. "With Kit, Age 7, at the Beach." In *Stories That Could Be True: New and Collected Poems by William Stafford*. New York: Harper & Row, 1977.

Teilhard de Chardin, Pierre. *On Suffering*. New York: Harper & Row, 1975.

Weatherhead, Leslie. *After Death*. New York and Nashville: Abingdon-Cokesbury Press, n.d.